ALIVE IN HIM

Devotionals by Caroline Stoerker
Journals by Ellie Krause

*But because of His great love for us, God, who is rich in
mercy, made us alive with Christ...*
(Ephesians 2:4-5)

Published by

ZOË LIFE
PUBLISHING
WORDS TO LIVE BY

Published by:
Zoë Life Publishing
P.O. Box 871066
Canton, MI 48187 USA
www.zoelifepub.com

Author: Caroline Stoerker and Journals by Ellie Krause
Illustrator: Lori Burton and The Zoe Life Creative Team
Editor: Zoe Life Editorial Team

First U.S. Edition 2012

Publisher's Cataloging-In-Publication Data

Stoerker, Caroline and Krause, Ellie

Summary: A whimsical look at the serious topic of learning to live for God through short stories, scriptures and practical application for pre-teens and young teens.

13 Digit ISBN 978-1-934363-71-3 soft cover

1.   Religion, Christianity, Youth Devotional, Ages 10 to 13

For current information about releases by Caroline Stoerker and Ellie Krause or other releases from Zoë Life Publishing, visit our website: http://www.zoelifepub.com.

Printed in the United States of America

#v7.2 4 5 2012

.

Evie Johnson

DEDICATION

This book is dedicated to my parents, Mark & Susan Stoerker, who have always encouraged me and helped me grow in my faith.

Caroline Stoerker

Caroline Stoerker
Phil 4:13

Ellie Krause

ALIVE IN HIM!
ACKNOWLEDGEMENTS

First, I would like to thank my parents for throwing so much support behind me so I could make my dream come true. They worked tirelessly and faithfully to help me, and they encouraged me when I doubted myself. Thanks to my sister, Catherine, for being the first person to read and critique the devotions. A big thank you to my nana who agreed to write the journals and to provide Biblical insight. I'd like to thank Jon & Sunny Williams, who gave me advice and feedback on my book and helped me get connected to the publishing world. A big thank-you goes to Merisa Davis, who instructed me on how to make an impression so I could get published and taught me how to navigate the complicated, adult-focused publishing world. Thank you to Sabrina Adams, who was my AMAZING publisher and made sure that the book was everything I dreamed about and more. Thanks to Zoe Life's creative team and the illustrator, Lori Burton, who created whimsical illustrations that were the perfect addition to the book. Thank you to all my friends & family who supported me and cheered me on the whole way. Finally, I would like to thank God for giving me this writing talent so that I could share His name with the world.

Caroline Stoerker

ALIVE IN HIM!
ACKNOWLEDGEMENTS

I would like to thank our gracious Heavenly Father for not only putting it in the heart of my granddaughter Caroline to write a devotional, but prompting her to ask for my help as well. What a joy!

Aware of my inability to begin this journey apart from the wisdom of the Lord, I asked for the prayers of others. My husband Don, my family, my friends and prayer partners in Rock Hill and Greenville, SC were faithful to lift both Caroline and me up in prayer.

A special thanks to the ladies in our Tuesday morning prayer group for the encouragement I received, and continue to receive, each week through their prayers.

Ellie Krause

ALIVE IN HIM

Devotionals by Caroline Stoerker
Journals by Ellie Krause

*But because of His great love for us, God, who is rich in
mercy, made us alive with Christ...*
(Ephesians 2:4-5)

Published by

ZOË LIFE
PUBLISHING
WORDS ✝ LIVE BY

TABLE OF CONTENTS

ALIVE IN HIM!
FOREWORD

As we have watched Caroline grow in her faith through the years, we are amazed at what God is doing in her life. It has been a joy and a privilege to see her grow not only physically but also spiritually. I remember the early days of teaching her the Scriptures and how she would memorize them. I remember how we would go for walks and she would ask what some might think a simplistic question but it would make us pause and think as we could tell she was so curious of the world around her.

We are thankful that we both had families that taught us and showed us God's love. It is amazing how we can learn and remember what our parents teach us- not only in words but also in actions. By sitting down and teaching us God's word, they have passed a legacy on to us.

We are humbled by the opportunity Caroline has been given to publish *Alive in Him*. We pray that God would use this book for His glory and to help you live for Him every day!

Mark and Susan Stoerker

SELF-CONTROL

Be self-controlled.
(1 Peter 5:8)

Sadie woke up and hopped out of bed one Tuesday morning, convinced the day would be a good one. She put on her slippers and headed downstairs for breakfast. Dad, her older brother, Nathan, and her younger brother, Will, were already downstairs making and eating breakfast.

"Morning, Sadie," Dad said. "We're making pancakes."

Sadie hungrily grabbed the pancake Nathan made for her. She wanted to put whipped cream on it, but none came out of the can. She glanced across the table at Will, who had a giant mound of whipped cream on his plate. Sadie felt like screaming at Will. She LOVED whipped cream and Will did not leave any for her, but she kept her mouth closed and ate her pancakes with just maple syrup.

After breakfast Sadie couldn't find her shoes because Will had hidden them. She finally found them just as the bus pulled up.

At school, Mr. Wylie announced that he had forgotten the cookies he promised to hand out to the fifth-graders.

Sadie felt like saying, *"What do you mean, you forgot? For three days in a row you told us you'd have them, and now you FORGET?!? Some teacher YOU are!"* She bit her tongue to keep quiet.

When Sadie opened her backpack, there was no lunch. *Oh no!* sighed Sadie. *Dad forgot to pack my lunch! Now I have to buy one of the yucky-blucky lunches from the cafeteria.* Sadie's dad had also forgotten to pack a note saying she'd ride home with the Millers, so she had to ride her normal bus home from school.

There was no snack waiting for Sadie on the table when she got home. Nathan had eaten it after discovering it was the last one. *That was my favorite snack,* Sadie sighed sadly as she pulled something else to eat out of the refrigerator.

Then closing the door, Sadie prayed silently. *Lord, thank you for helping me to hold my tongue today.*

LIVING OUT GOD'S WORD!

WORDS TO LIVE BY

Do to others as you would have them do to you.
(Luke 6:31)

*In your anger do not sin: Do not let the sun go down while
you are still angry...*
(Ephesians 4:26)

*Be self-controlled and alert. Your enemy the devil prowls
around like a roaring lion looking for someone to devour.*
(1 Peter 5:8)

ALIVE IN HIM!

DAY ONE: READ *SELF-CONTROL*

It was Tuesday and Sadie began the day, confident it would be a good one. But things did not turn out as she had hoped.

1. What did Sadie feel like doing at the breakfast table?

2. Why?

3. Can you relate to Sadie in any way? Explain.

DAY TWO: READ *SELF-CONTROL*

At school, Sadie looked forward to eating the cookies her teacher had promised to bring for her class. Again, she was disappointed!

1. Sadie's teacher made a promise to his class, but he did not keep it. Think back on the past few days; have you made a promise to someone and, like Mr. Wylie, have not done as you promised? If not, why not?

2. How can you keep from disappointing others? Refer to Luke 6:31 in this week's WORDS TO LIVE BY.

DAY THREE: READ *SELF-CONTROL*

Sadie experienced one disappointment after another; but each time she kept her emotions under control. You are not responsible for the actions of others, but you are accountable for your response.

1. How did Sadie honor God? Refer to Ephesians 4:26 and 1 Peter 5:8 in this week's WORDS TO LIVE BY.

DAY FOUR: READ *SELF-CONTROL*

The story *Self-Control* shows you that people, no matter how well meaning they are, will disappoint you.

1. Memorize 1 Peter 5:8.

DAY FIVE: *LIVE IT!*

1. Make a list of the areas in your life where you have been disappointed, but needed to show self-control. Like Sadie, it may be at mealtime, while at school, or in the home. It may involve your money, your effort, talents etc.

2. Pray over this list asking the Lord to help you be self-controlled in each of these areas.

PRAYER

Heavenly Father,

Thank You that with your help I can be self-controlled in the face of disappointment.

In Jesus' Name,
Amen

LIVING OUT GOD'S WORD!

_____

_____

_____

_____

_____

_____

_____

_____

_____

_____

_____

_____

_____

_____

_____

_____

_____

THE VIDEO PROJECT

*May the God who gives endurance and encouragement
give you a spirit of unity among yourselves
as you follow Christ Jesus.*
(Romans 15:5)

Nick was excited. He was working with his sister, Amy, Chandler, Drew and Grace on a video to present to their youth group. They had big plans for the video, but it was now Thursday and they were running out of time.

That night, Grace called Nick. "The group is getting together at Drew's place tomorrow morning to shoot the video. Can you come?"

"I can't," said Nick. "Bryson's clarinet recital is tomorrow morning, and I can't miss it. I'm sorry."

"OK," Grace replied. "There's also going to be another meeting Saturday afternoon at my house, too. I hope you can come to that."

"Alright," Nick replied. "Thanks for letting me know!" He hung up.

But on Saturday afternoon when Nick was at Grace's, he found that the group had already filmed the video—without him!

Nick felt left out. "Guys, we were working on this as a group," he reminded them.

"But you weren't here Friday," Chandler said. "And we were ready to film the video."

11

"I was supposed to film it!" Nick said angrily. "We all agreed that we'd work together on the movie."

"Let's see it," Grace said, trying to change the topic. "We didn't have a chance to watch it yesterday."

"Uh-oh," Grace said after they watched it. "The camera's really shaky, and you can't see Drew or me in some parts. We need to redo this. And since Nick wasn't there, Chandler had to give up his part so he could film. Let's do this again."

"But it's already 2:30!" Chandler cried. "We only have a few hours to get this to Pastor Rich!"

"He's right," Drew admitted. "Let's tell Pastor Rich that we couldn't get it together."

"Wait," Nick said. "Time isn't out completely. Let's pray and ask the Lord to help us. If we work together," Nick shot a glance at Chandler, "we can have this done. And since Pastor Rich lives down the street from me, I can get it to his house fast so we have a little more time. Let's stick to our parts."

"Yeah," Amy, Grace, Drew and even Chandler cheered. "We should have prayed before!"

"What were we thinking?" Grace said.

By 4:30, they had filmed the video, and it only took a few minutes to edit the mistakes. Nick got it to Pastor Rich's house an hour early, and on Sunday, the youth group was really impressed with their work.

"You see, guys?" Nick said. "Without the Lord's help, we would have not been able to get this video finished."

"You said it, dude!" Drew agreed.

LIVING OUT GOD'S WORD!

WORDS TO LIVE BY

May the God who gives endurance and encouragement give you a spirit of unity among yourselves as you follow Christ Jesus...
(Romans 15:5)

DAY ONE: READ *THE VIDEO PROJECT*

Nick was excited about his part in the production of a video for his youth group.

1. What is unity?

2. Who must give this unity to you? Refer to Romans 15:5 in this week's WORDS TO LIVE BY.

DAY TWO: READ *THE VIDEO PROJECT*

The unity of the group was disrupted when Nick was told the group had filmed the video without him. Nick felt left out and showed his disappointment by getting angry with Chandler.

1. Have you ever felt left out of a group project or left out of a social event?

2. How did you show your hurt?

LIVING OUT GOD'S WORD!

DAY THREE: READ *THE VIDEO PROJECT*

Grace, acting as the peacemaker, suggested they watch the video. After watching it, they realized it had to be re-done. But Drew and Chandler thought, *there's no way!*

1. Are you in a group situation where you feel like giving up? Why is this?

2. What will God give you if you ask? Refer to Romans 15:5 in this week's WORDS TO LIVE BY.

DAY FOUR: READ *THE VIDEO PROJECT*

Nick, Amy, Chandler, Drew and Grace began their project with excitement. But Chandler's unwillingness to wait until the whole group could get together disrupted their unity.

1. What characteristics are needed to have unity?

2. What is the result when unity is disrupted?

DAY FIVE: *LIVE IT!*

When you are working on a group project with others this week, stop and pray first that God would give you unity so your project can be completed. If you aren't working with a group on anything, pray and ask God that whenever you work with people in the future. He will give you unity.

PRAYER

Heavenly Father,

Thank you for the giving me opportunities to work with the other kids in my church. When I'm involved in a youth project, and problems arise, help me to remember it is You who gives us the spirit of unity.

In Jesus' Name,
Amen

LIVING OUT GOD'S WORD!

_____

_____

_____

_____

_____

_____

_____

_____

_____

_____

_____

_____

_____

_____

_____

_____

THE BRACELET 3

You shall not steal.
(Exodus 20:15)

Trish unfolded the money her mom had given her. It was five dollars to spend on whatever she pleased! Trish had her heart set on something from the jewelry store down the road, so she decided to go there to spend her money.

"Hi, Trish!" said Jessica, who was an employee at the store and Trish's very close friend. "Let me know if you need anything."

Trish waved. "Thanks, Jessica!" she said and then walked over to see the bracelet she wanted. It was a beaded bracelet with pink, blue, purple, and yellow beads and a charm with a peace sign on it. Trish looked at the price. "Ten dollars?!? I thought it would be on sale for five!" she groaned. She decided to get it anyway. *No one will know,* thought Trish, so when Jessica was helping another customer; Trish dropped the bracelet in her pocket and walked out of the store. When she arrived at her home, Trish put it on.

"Why Trish!" Mom exclaimed, "What a pretty bracelet! Did you buy it?"

"Um, uh, yeah, it was on sale," Trish fibbed, suddenly interested in the painting on the wall.

"Was Jessica there?" her mom asked. "Yeah," Trish answered.

"What did she say about the bracelet?"

"Mom, could you quit asking me stuff? I've got an article to read for homework."

At dinner, when Dad complimented on Trish's new bracelet, saying, "Nice bracelet, kiddo," Trish just pushed her peas around on her plate. "Um."

"Trish, is something going on?" Mom looked at her closely. "You've been acting funny ever since you got home."

Tears welled up in Trish's eyes as she answered. "I...I...I...stole the bracelet from the store. I didn't have enough money for it, so I took it."

"Trish," her dad said, "you know it is wrong to steal. You must return the bracelet and tell Jessica what you did. You sinned against God and should have never taken the bracelet."

Trish nodded as the tears spilled over. What had she done? She thought getting the bracelet would make her happy, but instead, Trish had landed in a whole lot of trouble with her parents. Now she had to tell Jessica what she did. Would Trish ever be able to face her again?

LIVING OUT GOD'S WORD!

WORDS TO LIVE BY

I have hidden your word in my heart that I might not sin against you.
(Psalm 119:11)

Honor your father and your mother, so that you may live long in the land the LORD your God is giving you.
(Exodus 20:12)

You shall not steal.
(Exodus 20:15)

You shall not give false testimony against your neighbor
(Exodus 20:16)

ALIVE IN HIM!

DAY ONE: READ *THE BRACELET*

Trish had her heart set on a bracelet at the jewelry store where her friend Jessica worked. But when Trish saw the price of the bracelet, her heart sank. She didn't have enough money to buy it, so she decided to steal it.

1. Has there been a time that you, like Trish, had your heart set on something but found you didn't have enough money to buy it? Explain.

2. What did you do?

DAY TWO: READ *THE BRACELET*

Trish did not put the bracelet on until she arrived home. When her mom saw it, she thought it was so pretty and wanted to know all about Trish's time at the store.

1. Which of God's commandments did Trish disobey when she answered her mom? Refer to Exodus 20: 12, 15 and 16 in this week's WORDS TO LIVE BY.

2. Have you disobeyed any one of these same commands when you answered a question that your mom or dad asked you? If so, which one? Why did you do this?

DAY THREE: READ *THE BRACELET*

During dinner, her mom realized that Trish was acting funny and asked what was going on. Tears welled up in Trish's eyes as she told her parents the truth about the bracelet. When her father told her what she must do, Trish learned that stealing does have consequences

1. Trish sinned against God. What does God tell us to do so that we might not sin against Him? Refer to Psalm 119:11 in this week's WORDS TO LIVE BY.

2. Memorize Exodus 20:15.

DAY FOUR: READ *THE BRACELET*

When Trish stole the bracelet she thought, *No one will know!* But Trish found she was wrong and suffered the consequences of her action. Breaking God's commandments may bring you happiness for a short time, but in the end it will produce shame and tears.

1. How might have the story ended if Trish had waited until she had enough money to buy the bracelet?

DAY FIVE: *LIVE IT!*

Whenever you are tempted to steal this week, stop and think of Trish. Pray that God will help you obey his commands. Refer to Exodus 20:15 in this week's WORDS TO LIVE BY.

PRAYER

Heavenly Father,

When I am tempted to take something that does not belong to me, help me to remember that You said, "You shall not steal." (Exodus 20:15).

In Jesus' Name,
Amen

LIVING OUT GOD'S WORD!

RULES

He who scorns instruction will pay for it, but he who respects a command is rewarded.
(Proverbs 13:13)

Erin sighed as she picked up the toys in her room. *If we didn't have that dumb rule about room cleaning, Erin thought, I would be at the pool with my friends right now.*

About that time Erin's stepmother, Alice entered the room and asked, "How's it going?"

"OK, I guess," Erin scowled. "Why do I have to pick up my room anyway?"

Alice answered, "You could trip over your toys and get hurt." Then Alice pointed to Erin's bed. "Don't shove everything under there or you'll be here longer." Erin sighed, but followed her stepmother's instructions.

After Erin finished cleaning her room, she went to the pool with her friends, Virginia and Alison. They decided to go over to the concession stand to get ice cream.

"Let's race," Erin suggested, and she and Virginia burst into a sprint to the stand. The lifeguard blew his whistle. "Walk, ladies!" Erin slowed down, but still walked fast.

After they ate their ice cream, Erin, Virginia, and Alison decided to go swimming.

"Since we can't have a race on the pool deck, let's have a swimming race," Erin suggested. Virginia and Alison agreed, and soon the girls were lined up at the shallow end. Out of the corner of her eye, Erin saw the NO DIVING sign, but deliberately ignored it. *What can happen to me?* Erin thought scornfully. When Alison announced, "GO!" Erin dove in the pool. Erin hit her head on the pool's concrete bottom, blacked out, and was rushed to the emergency room in critical condition.

Erin was in the hospital for three days before she was well enough to return home. When she got home, Alice asked her, "Now do you see why we have rules?"

Erin nodded. "We might not want to follow them, but rules are there for a reason. If I had followed the rules, I wouldn't have been in the hospital. From now on, I'm going to follow the rules."

LIVING OUT GOD'S WORD!

WORDS TO LIVE BY

Children, obey your parents in the Lord, for this is right.
(Ephesians 6:1)

He who scorns instruction will pay for it, but he who respects a command is rewarded.
(Proverbs 13:13)

DAY ONE: READ *RULES*

Erin thought the rule about room cleaning was dumb. But if she wanted to spend time at the pool with her friends, she had to pick up her room.

1. What rules have your parents made for you?

2. Do you feel the way as Erin about one of these rules? If so, which one?

DAY TWO: READ *RULES*

It is important to understand that the rules your parents put in place are for your good. Their rules are not suggestions, but commands and should be respected.

1. When you are tempted to argue with your parents about a rule, labeling it as dumb, what should you do instead? Refer to Ephesians 6:1 in this week's WORDS TO LIVE BY.

2. God gives commands to instruct us. What does the Bible say about the one who scorns (hates) instruction? Refer to Proverbs 13:13 in this week's WORDS TO LIVE BY.

DAY THREE: READ *RULES*

Erin's attitude toward rules was not only at home. She had that same attitude when she hung out with her friends, an attitude that put her in grave danger.

1. What is your attitude toward rules when you are hanging out with your friends? Is it the same as that when you are home?

2. Has this attitude kept you from getting hurt or, has it resulted in trouble for you? Explain.

DAY FOUR: READ *RULES*

Erin changed her attitude about rules only after getting hurt. The result of her choice to scorn instruction was very painful, but it turned out to be a great learning experience.

1. Rules are a part of life. Name a rule in a sport or in your school that you know is put in place for your protection.

2. What is your attitude toward that rule?

DAY FIVE: *LIVE IT!*

Today, make a list of the rules you have to follow. Pray over each one and ask God to help you follow the rules on your paper. Over the next week put a star beside each rule you obey. At the end of the week, reflect and thank God that He helped you to follow the rules!

PRAYER

Heavenly Father,

Thank you for giving me your commands to protect me. Please help me to think of them as my friends and not my enemies.

In Jesus' Name,
Amen

LIVING OUT GOD'S WORD!

ALIVE IN HIM!

PROMISES AND SECRETS

*A gossip betrays a confidence, but a
trustworthy man keeps a secret.*
(Proverbs 11:13)

"Promise you won't tell Chandler this," Nick whispered to Drew in the hall outside the gym.

"I won't, dude," Drew grinned.

"OK, then. Avery, Brian, Tommy, and I are throwing a big surprise party at the arcade for Chandler. No one else can know about it besides you and Chandler's friends, so keep it a secret."

Drew nodded and smiled. "You have my word."

At lunch later, Drew was tempted to tell Chandler about his party, but Drew held his tongue and remembered what Nick told him. "No one else can know," he silently repeated.

On the way to Brian's house for a party meeting, he ran into Chad Powell. "Where are you going?" Chad asked. Drew thought fast. "Um, I'm going to Brian's house. He got a new video game. You know, the cool war one." Chad smiled, nodded, and continued on his way.

"Have you told anyone yet?" Nick pounced on him as soon as he walked in the door.

"Nope," Drew grinned and shook his head.

Two days later as Drew was skateboarding with Evan, he thought, *I have to tell someone about this secret, If I don't I'll explode!* Then, giving into the temptation, Drew announced, "We're going to throw a big birthday party for Chandler. Just don't tell anyone, OK?"

"Alright," Evan agreed. Oops! Drew thought. *This time, I didn't hold my tongue—I let it slip!*

Later that night, Drew got a call from Nick. "Hello?" Drew said, but Nick started to yell. "Dude, I thought I could trust you. Now Chandler knows about his surprise birthday party because Evan told Chandler what you told him! You promised not to tell!"

"Look, I'm sorry," Drew replied, then pleaded, "Please forgive me."

But Nick stormed on. "We worked hard on that party, and now, the surprise is gone because of you! I'll never trust you again." He hung up, leaving Drew upset and guilty.

Drew sighed. How could he repair his friendship with Nick and the rest of the guys?

LIVING OUT GOD'S WORD!

WORDS TO LIVE BY

"Watch and pray so that you will not fall into temptation. The spirit is willing, but the body is weak."
(Matthew 26:41)

No temptation has seized you except what is common to man. And God is faithful; he will not let you be tempted beyond what you can bear. But when you are tempted, he will also provide a way out so that you can stand up under it.
(Corinthians 10:13)

A gossip betrays a confidence, but a trustworthy man keeps a secret.
(Proverbs 11:13)

If we confess our sins, he is faithful and just and will forgive us our sins and purify us from all unrighteousness.
(1 John 1:9)

Therefore, my brothers, I want you to know that through Jesus the forgiveness of sins is proclaimed to you.
(Acts 13:38)

Bear with each other and forgive whatever grievances you may have against one another. Forgive as the Lord forgave you.
(Colossians 3:13)

DAY ONE: READ *PROMISES AND SECRETS*

Drew was invited to join those who were planning a surprise birthday party for Chandler. He gave his Word that he would keep the party a secret.

1. That same day Drew was tempted to tell Chandler about the party, but held his tongue. Then, two days later while skateboarding with Evan, what did Drew feel he had to do?

2. Drew let the way he felt overrule what he knew was right. Have you ever done this? If so, why?

DAY TWO: READ *PROMISES AND SECRETS*

Soon after he promised to keep the party a secret, Drew felt the urge to tell others what had been told to him in confidence. The temptation to break his promise was not a sin, but Drew sinned when he gave into the temptation.

1. What should Drew have done the very moment he was tempted to tell Evan about the surprise birthday party? Refer to Matthew 26:41 in this week's WORDS TO LIVE BY.

2. What is the promise of God concerning temptation? Refer to 1 Corinthians 10:13 in this week's WORDS TO LIVE BY.

DAY THREE: READ *PROMISES AND SECRETS*

Nick's phone call later that night showed that Drew's action was not without consequences.

1. How did Drew's betrayal affect his relationship with Nick? What other harm did Drew's sin cause?

2. Memorize Proverbs 11:13.

DAY FOUR: READ *PROMISES AND SECRETS*

Drew sinned against God and against Chandler when he betrayed a confidence. Chandler refused to forgive Drew, even though Drew pleaded for forgiveness.

1. What does God promise if we confess our sins? Refer to 1 John 1:9 in this week's WORDS TO LIVE BY.

2. Through whom is God's forgiveness proclaimed? Refer to Acts 13:38 in this week's WORDS TO LIVE BY.

DAY FIVE: *LIVE IT!*

1. Have you trusted someone to keep a secret, then found out they had broken it?

2. Has the hurt of their betrayal been so deep that you couldn't forgive them?

3. Or, has your pride kept you from saying, "I forgive you?"

Write out Colossians 3:13, then ask the Lord to help you obey His Word.

PRAYER

Heavenly Father,

Thank you that when I confess my sins, you are faithful and just to forgive me.

Help me to forgive others in the same way.
And when I am tempted to betray a confidence, help me to remember that a trustworthy friend keeps a secret.

In Jesus' Name,
Amen

LIVING OUT GOD'S WORD!

_____

_____

_____

_____

_____

_____

_____

_____

_____

_____

_____

_____

_____

_____

_____

_____

_____

SELFISHNESS IN THE SNOW

Each of you should look not only to your own
interests, but also to the interests of others.
(Philippians 2:4)

Erin was ecstatic. It was a snow day, and there was tons of snow on the ground. School was canceled, and she had the whole day to spend with her neighbors, Virginia and Alison.

"Wanna come sledding with me?" Erin called and asked Virginia. "I'm going down to the big hill by the creek."

"OK," Virginia replied. "I'll call Alison and let her know."

Ten minutes later, the three girls were at the hill.

"Let's race," Alison suggested, and pushed down Erin's sled to get on it.

"Uh, Alison?" Erin said with a funny voice. "You and Virginia didn't bring sleds."

"Should I go back?" Virginia asked.

"Nah. We're fine," Erin said, and snatched the sled back from Alison and sled down the hill. "Whee! Hey, you guys, this is really awesome! This goes really fast."

After Erin sled down the hill four times, Alison and Virginia got bored.

"We haven't had a turn yet," Virginia complained. "We came to go sledding together, remember?"

"Deal with it," Erin replied sharply. "You didn't bring a sled, and I told you we were going sledding." She proceeded to continue sledding without a glance at Alison and Virginia.

After Erin's tenth time down the hill, Virginia turned to Alison. "Let's go," Virginia whispered. "We could probably have more fun at my house with Austin and Adam," Austin and Adam were Virginia's five-year-old brothers.

"Ditto," Alison replied, and the two of them left.

When Erin came back up the hill, there were no friends to be found. "Where'd they go?" she wondered. "I even built a ramp." She went home to call the girls to see where they went.

"Wanna build a snowman?" she called and asked Alison.

"I guess," Alison replied uncertainly, and soon the three were in Erin's yard, but Erin was the only one building the snowman. Virginia and Alison were off to the side.

"Do you need help?" Virginia asked as Erin struggled to put the head on the snowman.

"Nah. I can do it all by myself," Erin put the head on and stuck on the snowman's facial features. "Voila, ladies! My snowman!"

"We're going home now," Alison said grumpily.

"Why?" Erin asked. "We've had so much fun!"

"You're the only one that's having fun, Erin," Virginia explained. "You wouldn't let us take a turn on the sled at the hill, and you insisted on making the snowman all by yourself. You wouldn't let us do anything, and it's no fun spending the day with a person who won't share." The girls turned around and walked across the street.

"Wait!" Erin cried, but the girls ignored her. Erin slumped in the snow. What had she done? Why didn't she share? *I guess I did want everything to myself, Erin thought remorsefully. They're my friends, and I should have let them take a turn. Next time, I'll let them take a turn.*

✝

LIVING OUT GOD'S WORD!

WORDS TO LIVE BY

Each of you should look not only to your own interests, but also to the interests of others.

(Philippians 2:4)

My help comes from the LORD,
the Maker of heaven and earth.

(Psalm 121:2)

Help us, O God our Savior, for the glory of your name; deliver us and forgive our sins for your name's sake.

(Psalm 79:9)

DAY ONE: READ
SELFISHNESS IN THE SNOW

Erin was ecstatic when she heard that her school was cancelled because of the snow. Wasting no time, she arranged a sledding outing with two of her neighbors. Ten minutes later, they were on the big hill by the creek. The three girls were filled with excitement as they anticipated a day of fun in the snow.

1. Write Erin, Virginia, and Alison's names in a column. Then, next to each girl's name, characterize each one.

2. Which of the three girls do you identify with the most? Why?

DAY TWO: READ
SELFISHNESS IN THE SNOW

The expectations of Alison and Virginia were dashed when, instead of sledding, their time was spent on the sidelines, watching Erin go down the hill. When Virginia reminded her that they had come to go sledding together, Erin got ugly.

1. Why did Erin dishonor the Lord both in her attitude and actions? Refer to Philippians 2:4 in this week's WORDS TO LIVE BY.

2. Memorize Philippians 2:4.

DAY THREE: READ
SELFISHNESS IN THE SNOW

Clueless about the effect her behavior on Alison and Virginia, Erin initiated another activity. But again, it was all about Erin.

1. Erin was the one who initiated both activities with her friends but then, surprisingly, was the one who ignored them. Has there been a time when you initiated an activity, then ignored your friends? Explain.

2. Why did you behave in that way?

DAY FOUR: READ
SELFISHNESS IN THE SNOW

Erin had planned to spend the whole day with Alison and Virginia. But because she was rude and self-centered, they went home and Erin was left alone. At first she did not notice, but in the end it was very clear.

1. Have you ever been left alone because of your choices? Explain.

2. Who will help you make the right choices? Refer to Psalm 121:2 in this week's WORDS TO LIVE BY.

DAY FIVE: *LIVE IT!*

Until Alison and Virginia told her why they were leaving, Erin was clueless about the effect her behavior was having on her two friends. Erin thought they were having fun!

Their truthfulness made Erin reflect on her behavior and resolve to do better.

1. Thank the Lord for friends who are willing to be honest with you about your behavior.

2. Write out Psalm 79:9 and make it your personal prayer.

PRAYER

Heavenly Father,

Like Erin, I have a tendency to want everything to be all about me! And, like Erin, I can resolve to change. But I can't change without your help. Please help me to be one who looks only to that which interests me, but also to that which interests others.

In Jesus' Name,
Amen

LIVING OUT GOD'S WORD!

BAD INFLUENCES

A companion of fools suffers harm.
(Proverbs 13:20)

Sadie was so excited as she walked home from school one March afternoon. One month had passed since her family moved to Nebraska and Sadie FINALLY was able to find some girls with whom she could hang out.

"You seem excited, Sadie," said her little sister, Morgyn, when Sadie arrived at home.

"I am!" Sadie grinned. "Ashley, Jennifer, and Isabel let me sit with them at lunch! They seem so nice..."

They did seem pretty nice, Sadie thought, but I did heard Ashley using some bad words when talking to Jennifer and Isabel. I know it's foolish to talk like that, but I guess it won't hurt anything.

The next morning at school, Sadie found Jennifer and Isabel whispering by her locker, laughing really loud, and pointing to a boy who was walking by.

Isabel motioned for Sadie to come closer and whispered something mean about the boy, whose name was Joey, to Sadie. Jennifer started laughing and Sadie couldn't help but join in...she wanted the girls to accept her in their group so badly!

In biology class, Mr. Prince assigned a whole chapter review for homework! Sadie groaned under her breath, but wrote it down. She noticed Ashley refused to write the assignment down, but instead drew a cartoon of Mr. Prince with buckteeth.

In Language Arts, Sadie got bored, and imitating Ashley, drew a mean picture of her teacher. Only Sadie got caught and was given an extra page of homework.

At home that afternoon, Morgyn called to Sadie: "Hey sis, come help Mom and I with the laundry." Sadie groaned and said one of the swear words Ashley had used earlier.

"Sadie!" Mom came in just in time to hear the outburst. "That is not how we talk, young lady. Where did you pick that word up?"

"Well...from the girl I started to hang out with at school... she kinda uses those words," Sadie admitted.

"Honey," Mom sighed, "she sounds like a foolish young girl. Hanging out with her has already done you more harm than good."

Mom's right! thought Sadie. Then she said, "I won't hang out with her or her friends anymore!"

LIVING OUT GOD'S WORD!

WORDS TO LIVE BY

He who walks with the wise grows wise, but a companion of fools suffers harm.

(Proverbs 13:20)

Do not be misled: "Bad company corrupts good character."

(I Corinthians 15:33)

DAY ONE: READ *BAD INFLUENCES*

Sadie was so excited! After living in Nebraska for one month, she finally found some girls she could hang out with.

1. What was Sadie willing to compromise because she desperately wanted these girls to accept her?

2. What have you compromised in order to *fit in*?

DAY TWO: READ *BAD INFLUENCES*

Sadie's choice of friends was affecting who she was as a person. She was growing up in a house where she was taught the difference between right and wrong. Sadie knew it was wrong to use bad language, make fun of people, and to disrespect authority. However, based on her choice of friends, Sadie turned her back on what she knew was right, deliberately choosing what she knew was wrong instead.

1. What must you keep in mind as you choose the boys and girls you want to hang out with? Refer to Proverbs 13:20 and I Corinthians 1:33 in this week's WORDS TO LIVE BY.

DAY THREE: READ *BAD INFLUENCES*

Sadie's story shows us the importance of choosing our friends wisely. The people we hang out with will have either a good influence on us, or a bad one. Friendships are never stagnant.

1. Before long, Sadie was imitating Ashley's behavior. What were the results?

2. Memorize Proverbs 13:20.

DAY FOUR: *READ BAD INFLUENCES*

Sadie's mom confronted her daughter about her behavior, but she did it in a loving way.

1. How did Sadie respond?

2. How do you respond when you are asked to explain your behavior to your parents?

DAY FIVE: *LIVE IT!*

Make a list of your friends—the ones you talk with on the phone, play with, or hang out with at school. Write down the characteristics of each one. Are you imitating any of your friends' behavior? If so, in what way? If you are imitating them in a bad way, pray and ask God to help you find friends that are good influences.

PRAYER

Heavenly Father,

Please help me to choose friends that obey your word, friends that do not talk or act in a way that is not good for me, or for them.

In Jesus' Name,
Amen

LIVING OUT GOD'S WORD!

_____

_____

_____

_____

_____

_____

_____

_____

_____

_____

_____

_____

_____

_____

_____

_____

_____

TRACK TRYOUTS

Do not be anxious about anything, but in everything, by prayer and petition, with thanksgiving, present your requests to God. And the peace of God, which transcends all understanding, will guard your hearts and your minds in Christ Jesus.
(Philippians 4:6-7)

"Are you trying out for the track team?" Nick asked Drew during locker break.

"I want to," Drew twirls the combination on his locker and the door pops opens. "But there's so many other kids that are faster. Have you seen Jordan run in gym? He's amazing!"

"You really should try out," Nick said. "You're so good."

The truth was, Drew loved running. He wanted to try out for the team, but he doubted he would make it. Besides, Jordan would be a much better person for Coach Schultz's team.

Drew couldn't get it off his mind, not even while they were conducting an experiment in science, his favorite class besides gym. "Hey," whispered Anna Kate, his lab partner. "You're not paying attention!"

Drew paid no attention to what Anna Kate said. He was too busy thinking about whether he should try out for the team. *I probably won't make it, but I really should try out,* Drew said to himself as he signed his name on the clipboard.

"I signed up to try out for the track team, but I don't think I'll make it, Dad," Drew said after school. "Jordan is so much better than me. He'll probably outrun me by a mile! I'm not going to do good AT ALL. I need some help!"

"Drew, why are you so anxious? You are a great runner!" Dad said as he took a Coke out of the refrigerator. "Son, thank the Lord that you can run, then ask Him to give you peace about the tryouts."

Drew sighed as he turned and went up the stairs to his room.

The next day Drew showed up at the field for tryouts. He saw Jordan walking over and he gulped. *This will be some serious competition,* he thought. *But Jordan will win.*

Coach Schultz blew the whistle. "Alright, boys! I want you to run two laps around the field as fast as you can. Go!"

Sprinting off, Drew thought, *This is great!* The wind blowing against his face as he passed many of the boys. Jordan was the only one standing between him and the team. Drew kept running, anyway, and didn't mind when he happened to be the fourth to finish.

That night, though, Drew became even more anxious. Would he make the team? The principal was announcing the results over the intercom, so the whole school would know if he made it. He was so worried that he couldn't go to sleep! Then Drew remembered what his dad had told him and prayed, *Lord, thank you that I was able to try out for the track team. Please help me not to worry about the results.* Then Drew fell asleep.

The next day, the principal came on the intercom. "Many boys tried out for the team, but only have a few spots open," she announced. She started reading a list of names; "Jordan," Of course, Drew thought. "Ryan, Aaron..." The principal kept reading. She came to the last couple names: "Brian, and Drew!"

LIVING OUT GOD'S WORD!

WORDS TO LIVE BY

*Do not be anxious about anything, but in everything, by
prayer and petition, with thanksgiving,
present your requests to God.*
(Philippians 4:6)

*And the peace of God, which transcends all understanding,
will guard your hearts and your minds in Christ Jesus.*
(Philippians 4:7)

DAY ONE: READ *TRACK TRYOUTS*

Nick and Drew were talking during locker break. When Nick asked if Drew was planning to try out for the track team, Drew said he wanted to, but doubted that he could make it.

1. Have you wanted to try out for something, but hesitated to do so?

2. Why did you hesitate?

DAY TWO: READ *TRACK TRYOUTS*

Encouraged by Nick, Drew signed up to try out for the track team. But instead of thinking, *I'm going to try my best to win;* Drew's thoughts were focused on the abilities of those he was competing against.

1. What did Drew's dad say Drew should do?

2. How did Drew respond?

3. When have you been instructed in God's Word and then, like Drew, just sighed and walk away?

DAY THREE: READ *TRACK TRYOUTS*

When the time for the tryouts came, Drew showed up and competed. He was the fourth to finish. Would he make the team? That night Drew was so worried that he couldn't go to sleep. Then, he remembered what his dad had told him, and Drew prayed.

1. What was Drew able to do after he prayed?

2. Drew thanked the Lord that he was able to try out for the track team. Will you pray when you go to bed tonight and, like Drew, thank the Lord for something you were able to do today?

DAY FOUR: READ *TRACK TRYOUTS*

When he learned there were tryouts for the track team, Drew spent most of his time worrying about Jordan, one of the runners he would be competing against. "Jordan is so much better than me," Drew told his father. "I'm not going to do good AT ALL!" Drew's anxiety only increased his lack of confidence.

1. What does God say we should do instead of worrying? Refer to Philippians 4:6 in this week's WORDS TO LIVE BY.

2. What will God give you to guard your heart and mind against anxiety? Refer to Philippians 4:7 in this week's WORDS TO LIVE BY.

DAY FIVE: *LIVE IT!*

1. Memorize Philippians 4:6-7.

2. When you are given an opportunity to try out for something or you are asked to participate in an activity in the next few days, ask the Lord to guard your mind with His peace so that you do not become anxious.

3. Write down the difference in your attitude.

PRAYER

Heavenly Father,

Help me not to worry about anything, but to pray about everything.

In Jesus' Name,
Amen

LIVING OUT GOD'S WORD!

TRISH'S CHORES

Do everything without complaining or arguing.
(Philippians 2:14)

It was a beautiful Saturday morning and Trish couldn't wait to start riding her bike with Kara and Luke, her next-door neighbors. As Trish started to rush out the door, Mom stopped her. "Whoa, whoa, whoa, Trish," she said. "Have you done your chores?"

"No, but..." Trish stated.

"But nothing," her mom said. "You have to do your chores."

Trish's first chore was feeding the cat. Easy enough! She looked at the next item on the list. "Dusting the kitchen blinds?!?" Trish cried. "Awwww!"

"Why do I have to do this?" Trish complained. "It's boring! Ewwww, there's a dead bee!" Trish screamed, knocking the bee with her duster into the garbage can. "I hate dusting!"

"If you keep complaining, you won't get any allowance." Trish's mom warned. Trish grimaced, but she managed to keep quiet until she finished dusting.

But Trish began to grumble again when she looked on the list and saw that she had to clean her room. "Cleaning my room? Man! I bet Kara doesn't have to clean her room! Mom, can I skip this?"

"No," was her mom's reply.

The final item on her list was washing and drying the dishes. "I hate doing dishes," Trish yelled as she carelessly plunged a plate into the dishwater. Immediately she heard a shattering noise. "Oh, no!" Trish cried.

"Trish!" exclaimed Mom from the dining room. "Come here."

As Trish shuffled into the dining room, Mom asked, "What did I tell you would happen if you kept complaining about your chores?"

"I wouldn't get my allowance," Trish answered.

"Correct," Mom said. "As for the plate you broke, it cannot be fixed, but your attitude can."

It already has, thought Trish. *I've learned my lesson!*

WORDS TO LIVE BY

Do everything without complaining or arguing.
(Philippians 2:14)

DAY ONE: READ *TRISH'S CHORES*

One beautiful Saturday morning Trish started to rush out the door when her mom stopped her. Trish had not done her chores.

1. What chores must you do before you are allowed to play?

2. When have you, like Trish, tried to get away without doing them?

DAY TWO: READ *TRISH'S CHORES*

Trish was not a happy camper! She didn't like doing chores and Trish showed her dislike for them by arguing and complaining as she worked. After receiving a warning from her mom, Trish managed to keep quiet, but not for long.

1. Do you hate any of your chores? If so, which one?

2. Do you show that attitude while doing that chore? If so, how?

3. What warning, if any, have you been given?

DAY THREE: READ *TRISH'S CHORES*

Trish's hatred for her chores grew as she worked. She became careless while washing dishes and broke a plate. Trish's mom followed through with her warning and Trish paid for failing to listen.

1. What did Trish's attitude toward her chores cost her?

2. Can you relate to Trish in any way? If so, how?

DAY FOUR: READ *TRISH'S CHORES*

Trish didn't think her friend Kara had to clean her room, so Trish asked her mom if she could skip that chore. Her mom said, "No." If Trish hoped to change her mom's mind by her constant complaining, it didn't work.

1. How should Trish have done her work?

2. Memorize Philippians 2:14.

ALIVE IN HIM!

DAY FIVE: *LIVE IT!*

Today, ask the Lord to help you do one of your chores that you really dislike without complaining or arguing.

Write down the difference in your attitude.

PRAYER

Heavenly Father,

Please help me to do everything without complaining or arguing.

In Jesus' Name,
Amen

LIVING OUT GOD'S WORD!

THE TONGUE

Set a guard over my mouth, O LORD; keep watch over the door of my lips.
(Psalm 141:3)

Amy peeked over at her brother Nick's picture.

"That's a sorry hot air balloon," Amy said. "Here. Let me show you how to do one." She started to draw on a spare piece of paper.

"Well, at least mine is more colorful than yours!" Nick retorted after seeing Amy draw for a few minutes. "And yours is smaller!"

"Shut up!" Amy growled. "At least my people aren't sticks!"

"At least I have the markers!" Nick taunted, snatching the marker box.

"Give it back, stupid!" Amy cried.

"Stupid yourself," Nick started coloring, satisfied with himself.

Amy peered at Nick, thinking of a mean trick to get the markers back. "Hey, Nick!" she exclaimed. "There's a big bug out the window!"

"Where?" Nick asked. He looked out the window. Amy took the marker box.

"Hey!" cried Nick.

"Ha ha," said Amy. "You actually fell for that? You are so dumb!"

"Whatever," Nick said. "At least I'm smarter than you! Did you see my report card? What now?"

"You little..." Amy stopped because Dad had come into the kitchen.

"Kids!" he cried. "Why are you fighting?"

"She called me dumb and stupid and told me to shut up!" Nick yelled.

"Well he said mean things to me!" Amy cried. This led to another fight, which lasted for another few minute.

"Hey, hey, hey," Dad said, stepping between them. "You both said mean things, so now you're both in trouble. Your words aren't the nicest things. The tongue is a strong weapon; it can start a fire quickly. Next time, use your tongue for good."

LIVING OUT GOD'S WORD!

WORDS TO LIVE BY

A gentle answer turns away wrath,
but a harsh word stirs up anger.
(Proverbs 15:1)

When we put bits into the mouths of horses to make them
obey us, we can turn the whole animal. Or take ships as
an example. Although they are so large and are driven
by strong winds, they are steered by a very small rudder
wherever the pilot wants to go. Likewise the tongue is a
small part of the body, but it makes great boasts. Consid-
er what a great forest is set on fire by a small spark. The
tongue also is a fire, a world of evil among the parts of the
body. It corrupts the whole person, sets the whole course of
his life on fire, and is itself set on fire by hell.
(James 3:3-6)

All kinds of animals, birds, reptiles and creatures of the sea
are being tamed and have been tamed by man, but no man
can tame the tongue. It is a restless evil,
full of deadly poison.
(James 3:7-8)

Set a guard over my mouth, O LORD; keep watch over the
door of my lips.
(Psalm 141:3)

ALIVE IN HIM!

DAY ONE: READ *THE TONGUE*

Amy and her brother Nick were sitting together in their kitchen coloring. But before long, the two of them were fighting. The fighting ended when their dad came in and stood between them.

1. What stirred up the anger in Amy and Nick? Refer to Proverbs 15:1 in this week's WORDS TO LIVE BY.

2. Name a time that you began a fun activity with a sibling or a friend and ended hurling insults at one another.

DAY TWO: READ *THE TONGUE*

1. Make a list of the unkind things you have said to your sibling(s), parents and/or friends.

2. Read over the list. What are you thinking as you read it? Would you want to be your friend?

DAY THREE: READ *THE TONGUE*

James 3:3-6 compares the tongue to a very small rudder on a large ship, a bit in the mouth of horses and a tiny spark that can set a great forest on fire.

These comparisons show the tongue has both the power to control and the power to destroy. Then, in verses 7-8, a contrast is drawn concerning the taming of the tongue.

1. What contrast does God make? Refer to James 3:7-8 in this week's WORDS TO LIVE BY.

2. Look up the word tame in the dictionary. What does it mean?

DAY FOUR: READ *THE TONGUE*

Amy and Nick's dad said they should use their tongue for good.

1. Who must the children look to for the help to obey their dad? Refer to Psalm 141:3 in this week's WORDS TO LIVE BY.

2. Memorize Psalm 141:3.

DAY FIVE: *LIVE IT!*

When you are tempted to say something mean this week, seek God's help before you speak. He will set a guard over your mouth if you ask Him.

PRAYER

Heavenly Father,

When I am tempted to say something unkind, remind me to pray, "Set a guard over my mouth, O LORD; keep watch over the door of my lips."

In Jesus' Name,
Amen

LIVING OUT GOD'S WORD!

THE CHEATER

*Do not merely listen to the word, and so deceive your-
selves. Do what it says.*
(James 1:22)

Alison yawned as she got out of bed. Time for another long
day at school! She rubbed her eyes and looked at her planner on her night stand to see if she had any assignments.
Her eyes nearly popped out of her head when she saw SO-
CIAL STUDIES TEST—FRIDAY! It was Thursday! Alison
needed to make an A on this test or she wouldn't make the
honor roll for the first quarter. She had to figure out some
way to score an A!

On the way down the hall, Alison passed Chandler, a
straight A student in social studies. He had never even made
a B on anything in social studies and knew all the material
so well!

"Chandler!" Alison called, beckoning for him to come over
to her locker. "Got a favor to ask!"

"What?" he said.

"I need you to give me the answers to the social studies
test tomorrow," Alison said. "You'll get two weeks of my allowance. Please!"

Chandler paused a moment, then said, "OK. Listen, I'll
put the answers in your locker in between fourth and fifth
period. What's your locker combo?"

"Thirty-five, seven, ten," Alison recited.

Right before fifth period PE, Alison stopped by her locker

and found the answers to the social studies test! YES! Now she didn't need to study!

Friday morning, Alison used the cheat sheet Chandler gave her for the test. She got an A+ and made the honor roll! Alison was excited, but a little feeling deep inside her said, *What you did was wrong, Alison.* Alison ignored it. No one really would ever find out!

But three weeks later—the day of the honor roll celebration—the feeling was stronger. Sadly, Alison accepted her certificate. *I really didn't earn this, she thought. I guess I should tell!*

After the ceremony, Alison went up to her social studies teacher. "Mrs. Dawkinson?" she said. "I have something I have to tell you." She poured out the whole story.

"Thank you for being honest, Alison, but I will have to give you a zero on the test for cheating and I will have to take away your privileges as an honors student as well."

Alison nodded, tears in her eyes. Why had she cheated?

WORDS TO LIVE BY

Nothing in all creation is hidden from God's sight. Every-
thing is uncovered and laid bare before the eyes
of him to whom we must give account.
(Hebrews 4:13)

Do not merely listen to the word, and so deceive yourselves.
Do what it says.
(James 1:22)

Anyone who listens to the word but does not do what it says
is like a man who looks at his face in a mirror
and, after looking at himself, goes away and immediately
forgets what he looks like.
(James 1:23-24)

But the man who looks intently into the perfect law that
gives freedom, and continues to do this, not forgetting
what he has heard,
but doing it—he will be blessed in what he does.
(James 1:25)

DAY ONE: READ *THE CHEATER*

Alison needed an A in social studies to make the honor roll for the first quarter.

1. What was Alison willing to give up so she wouldn't have to study for her test?

2. Name a time when you have given up something you have in return for something you knew was wrong. Explain.

DAY TWO: READ *THE CHEATER*

Alison used the cheat sheet Chandler gave her, got an A+ and made the honor roll. She was excited, but deep inside, Alison knew what she did was wrong.

1. What are some reasons why Alison chose to ignore her conscience?

2. Why do you deceive yourself when you think, No one will know? Refer to Hebrews 4:13 in this week's WORDS TO LIVE BY.

DAY THREE: READ *THE CHEATER*

After accepting her certificate at the honor roll celebration, Alison's conscience would not allow her to keep silent. She poured out the whole story to her teacher.

1.   What did Alison's deception cost her?

2.   Memorize James 1:22.

DAY FOUR: READ *THE CHEATER*

Alison deceived herself when she decided to cheat in school.

1.   What is the person like who listens to the Word but does not do what it says? Refer to James 1:23-24 in this week's WORDS TO LIVE BY.

2.   What does God promise the one who continues to obey His word? Refer to James 1:25 in this week's WORDS TO LIVE BY.

DAY FIVE: *LIVE IT!*

In the next few days when you are tempted to take the easy way out; stop and think: Am I deceiving myself?

PRAYER

Heavenly Father,

Help me not to be one who merely listens to your word; but one who does what it says.

In Jesus' Name,
Amen

LIVING OUT GOD'S WORD!

_____

_____

_____

_____

_____

_____

_____

_____

_____

_____

_____

_____

_____

_____

_____

_____

_____

REVENGE

*You have heard that it was said, Love your neighbor
and hate your enemy. But I tell you:
Love your enemies and pray for
those who persecute you.*
(Matthew 5:43-44)

Grace skipped down the sixth-grade hall heading to her sixth period class—Social Studies, with Mrs. Dubois, who was her favorite teacher. Nothing could change her happy mood! She had gotten A's on both her math and language arts finals, and in band, she got a good grade for her testing song. PE was actually fun—they had played basketball—and during study hall, Grace's class was reading one of her favorite books. Only two periods left to go, and in seventh period, they were having a pep rally for the football team.

Just as Grace reached her locker, she fell to the ground, books flying everywhere. Kids laughed and pointed, and when Grace got up, she saw Trish and Carla standing in front of her, snickering. Grace knew they had tripped her, and she fumed with anger, but didn't let it show.

Social Studies was good—Grace got another A on her finals—and then came the pep rally. The pep rally had fun games, like races to see if you could beat the football players in a lap around the gym. Grace and another girl, Sadie, were selected to race. Grace was ahead of everyone except one football player. She let out a burst of speed and passed the football player, but didn't notice Trish was on the front row of the bleachers, subtly sticking out her foot.

WHOMP! Grace hit the gym floor as the other racers dashed in front of her. Everyone hooted with laughter. Now Grace was really mad. How dare Trish make her look like a fool in front of the entire school!

"I'm going to do something," Grace confided in her best friend, Ivy, after school.

"Like what?" Ivy asked as they rounded the corner and turned onto Spring Street.

"Like something so bad, Trish will totally regret messing with me. Think revenge here, Ivy," Grace snickered.

The girls walked down Spring Street in silence for a while, then Grace spoke. "I've got it! I sit in the back row in the last seat in social studies in the very corner of the room. Trish sits in front of me, and I can do something like, stick gum in her hair!"

The next day, at the end of social studies, Grace popped a piece of watermelon super-sticky gum in her mouth and chewed quickly. She placed it gently on Trish's long, black hair. When the bell rang, everyone started snickering. Trish thought they were laughing at someone else, but when she reached to pull her hair up in a ponytail, her hand landed on a wad of gum.

"EEW! Gross! Gum! Oh, help me get it out!" Trish shrieked, trying to pull it out. The gum wouldn't move. "OUCH!"

"What's going on?" Mrs. Dubois came into the hallway. "Trish, are you alright?"

Trish wordlessly pointed to the gum in her hair.

It didn't take a rocket scientist to figure out Grace had done it. Grace sat behind Trish in social studies, and Grace was also the only one trying not to laugh.

"But…" Grace tried to explain in the vice principal's office, "she tripped me not once, but twice…"

"Grace," he said, "that was a cruel joke. Revenge is frowned upon here at Pondwell Middle School. I'm afraid I will have to punish you. What you did was unacceptable."

Grace hung her head. She thought she was doing the right thing, but she really wasn't. I guess revenge isn't the best solution, she thought sadly.

WORDS TO LIVE BY

Do not say, "I'll do to him as he as done to me. I'll pay that man back for what he did."
(Proverbs 24:29)

DAY ONE: READ *REVENGE*

Grace was in a happy mood as she skipped down the hall. Her mood quickly changed, however, when she fell down, tripped on purpose by two girls who were standing in front of her locker. Grace chose not to let her anger show.

1. When have you been angry with someone but chose not to show it?

2. Did you think about getting even?

DAY TWO: READ *REVENGE*

Grace's anger toward Trish grew even more intense when Trish tripped her again. This time Grace was in a race at the pep rally and she fell in front of the entire school.

1. How did Grace decide to get even with Trish?

2. Who did Grace tell about her plan?

3. How should have Ivy reacted to Grace's plan of revenge?

DAY THREE: READ *REVENGE*

When Grace carried out her plan to put gum in Trish's hair, things didn't turn out as Grace hoped. The class snickered when they saw the gum, but it was Grace who got in trouble.

1. When did Grace find out that revenge was not the best solution to her anger against Trish?

DAY FOUR: READ *REVENGE*

Grace was a student whose anger toward Trish was not apparent to others until Trish tripped her a second time. Revenge seemed like the best solution to Grace's anger.

1. When have you thought the best way to handle your anger was to get even?

2. What did you decide to do?

3. Did you carry out your plan? If so, what happened?

DAY FIVE: *LIVE IT!*

The Word of God has a lot to say about personal revenge. When we fail to seek God's will and, like Grace, do what we think is best, we find we were wrong.

1.   Memorize Proverbs 24:29.

PRAYER

Heavenly Father,

Help me not to seek revenge. Instead, help me to seek You and to and ask for Your help to obey Your Word.

In Jesus' Name,
Amen

LIVING OUT GOD'S WORD!

FEUDING FRIENDS

A friend loves at all times.
(Proverbs 17:17)

Erin, Alison, and Virginia were having a sleep over at Erin's house one Saturday night. They were eating popcorn, drinking Coke, and listening to pop music on Virginia's iPod. They were having so much fun, but they didn't know that their sleep over was about to turn ugly...

It started when Alison got up to use the bathroom. Erin took this opportunity to tell Virginia about a rumor Erin had heard during locker break on Friday.

"Virginia, did you hear about Alison?" Erin whispered, keeping an eye on the closed bathroom door.

Virginia shook her head. "Nope. Tell me about it!"

Erin leaned in. "Well, Sydney told me that Alison tripped another kid in the cafeteria and then cheated off him on the science test Thursday. The kid is really smart, and Alison got away with everything. She ended up with an A on the science test, and the poor kid didn't even know about the cheating," Erin informed Virginia.

Virginia gasped. "Oh, my goodness! Alison would never, ever do such a thing! She's so nice to everyone."

"Or is she?" Erin challenged. "Cheating and tripping isn't nice."

"But that can't be true!" Virginia forgot about keeping quiet and started to yell at her friend. "That's a rumor. Sydney always lies!"

"No, she doesn't!" Erin yelled back. "Janie was right there with us, and she agreed with Sydney!"

"Sydney and Janie are best friends," Virginia retorted. "And Alison is a nice person!"

"She's a bad person," Erin's eyes flashed. "And on Monday, I plan to tell Mrs. Chandler that Alison cheated on the test and pushed the same kid she cheated off of down."

"What if it's not true?" a quiet voice interjected. Both Virginia and Erin whirled around to see Alison, standing quietly and sadly outside the bathroom door.

"It isn't," Virginia exclaimed as Erin jumped up to face Alison.

"Erin, I never would do that," Alison continued. "Sydney lied to you."

"Oh, Alison! I'm so sorry. I should have...." Erin tried to hug Alison, but Alison stepped away.

"Erin, it doesn't matter anymore," Alison said quietly. Her lower lip was quivering, and Virginia could tell Alison was trying not to cry. "I'm calling my mom and going home." She picked up her duffel bag and walked out the door, pressing buttons on her cellphone as she walked.

Virginia shot Erin a disgusted look. "What were you thinking?"

Erin sadly laid down on her sleeping bag. She had just lost one of her very best friends, and had fought with another. What could happen next?

WORDS TO LIVE BY

Love is patient, love is kind. It does not envy, it does not boast, it is not proud. It is not rude, it is not self-seeking, it is not easily angered, it keeps no record of wrongs. Love does not delight in evil but rejoices with the truth. It always protects, always trusts, always hopes, always perseveres.

(1 Corinthians 13:4-7)

Hear, O LORD, my righteous plea; listen to my cry. Give ear to my prayer—it does not rise from deceitful lips.

(Proverbs 17:17)

DAY ONE: READ *FEUDING FRIENDS*

This is a story about conflict among friends.

1. What is a friend?

2. What does God say a friend should do? Refer to Proverbs 17:17 in this week's WORDS TO LIVE BY.

DAY TWO: READ *FEUDING FRIENDS*

The conflict in the story took place when Erin was not a loving friend. The Bible says, "A friend loves at all times."

1. What is love? Refer to 1 Corinthians 13:4-7 in this week's WORDS TO LIVE BY.

2. Look at 1 Corinthians 13:4-7 again. Describe a time when you showed one of these acts of love to a friend.

DAY THREE: READ *FEUDING FRIENDS*

Erin needs to realize what it means to be a friend. Think about the way you treat your friends.

1. Which character are you most like: Erin or Virginia?

2. Which one of these girls should you be like?

DAY FOUR: READ *FEUDING FRIENDS*

Instead of talking behind her back, Erin should have asked Alison if what she heard at school was true.

1. Have you ever talked about your friends behind their back?

2. If so, why, and how did it affect your relationship?

DAY FIVE: *LIVE IT!*

Today, ask God that He would help you become a friend that is loyal and loves at all times. Then, if you ever have been an unloving friend, ask forgiveness of your friend.

PRAYER

Heavenly Father,

Thank You for the friends You have given me. Please give me the courage to defend my friends. And when I'm tempted to talk about my friends behind their back, help me to resist. Make me a friend who loves at all times.

In Jesus' Name,
Amen

PUTTING THINGS OFF

*There is a time for everything and a
season for every activity
under heaven.*
(Ecclesiastes 3:1)

"Boys and girls, listen up," Ms. Bertelli tried to get the class to quiet down. "You have a book report due this Friday, and it has to be at least three pages long. It can be on any book of your choice, but the topic must be school appropriate and the book must be on your reading level." Several boys groaned.

"If you have any questions, come see me after class."

Sadie made a note in her planner about the report as the bell rang, signaling the end of class. She had to get cracking on the report as soon as she got home, otherwise, she'd never have it done by Friday!

When she got home that afternoon, Sadie had a quick snack, then started on her homework. Before she had a chance to get to the report, however, her new friend Cayden called wanting to play an online game. Sadie agreed, and she spent until dinner time playing the game. After dinner, she had chores.

Tuesday was a typical day at school. Ms. Bertelli reminded them about the report. Sadie made a mental note to check out the book from the library, but she forgot all about it when Mom took her shopping for new running shoes.

Wednesday was an early release day, so Sadie would have more time to work. She checked out the book and read it, but just as she was about to start her rough draft, Cayden called. "Let's go to the skating rink," she said. Sadie went, and then had dinner with Cayden's family, so she didn't get back until around 8:00pm.

Thursday, Sadie had less homework than usual, but she also had Girl Scouts.

When she got home, her mom said, "Ms. Bertelli sent an e-mail reminding your class about the book report due tomorrow. Have you finished yours?"

Sadie hung her head. "I haven't even started it. I was planning to, I really was but...but...I put it off so I could have fun with my friends."

Mom sighed. "Well, Sadie, you have a lot of work to do. Better get started."

Sadie spent many hours working on her report and finally finished. When English class rolled around on Friday, Sadie handed it in. She hoped that she'd get a good grade, but because she put it off, she knew that the chances were slim. She really needed more time to work on it.

On Monday, Sadie was so nervous about how Ms. Bertelli would react that she had to go to the nurse. Even though she got to rest a little bit, she was still nervous.

"Many of you did exceptionally well on this report," Ms. Bertelli announced later. "I was very pleased with some of the reports, but others weren't very good at all; I could see the lack of effort in the reports. Make sure you're putting your 100% best into your work. Oh, and Sadie, I'd like to see you after class."

Five minutes later, Sadie stood by Ms. Bertelli's desk. The teacher held up Sadie's report, with a big red C at the top. Sadie gulped when she saw it!

"Sadie, I'm disappointed in you. You do much better work than this. What happened?"

"I'm really sorry," Sadie replied. "I knew that I should get the book report done, but I put it off until the very last possible minute."

Uncomfortable silence hung in the air, and then the bell rang again, signaling the start of the next class. Ms. Bertelli dismissed Sadie with a "thank-you" for being honest.

Sadie ran out of the classroom. Then she headed to the next class with a sigh of regret, *I never should have put off my homework!*

WORDS TO LIVE BY

There is a time for everything, and a season for every activity under heaven:
(Ecclesiastes 3:1)

My dear brothers, take note of this: Everyone should be quick to listen, slow to speak and slow to become angry.
(James 1:19)

DAY ONE: READ *PUTTING THINGS OFF*

Sadie had a book report due on Friday and intended to start working on it right away, but that did not happen!

1. What reason did Sadie give when her mom asked if she had finished the book report?

2. Name a time when instead of doing your homework, you spent time doing what you wanted to do.

DAY TWO: READ *PUTTING THINGS OFF*

It was Thursday evening before Sadie began working on her book report. She worked hard and completed it, but realized she only had a slim chance to get a good grade. Sadie needed more time, but the time had run out!

1. What are you putting off, thinking, I'll have time to work on that later?

2. Memorize Ecclesiastes 3:1.

DAY THREE: READ *PUTTING THINGS OFF*

Apparently Sadie's friend, Cayden, did not have any homework or it was not a priority.

1. Do your friends have the same priorities as you? If not, why not?

2. Why is it important for you to have friends who have the same priorities as you?

DAY FOUR: READ *PUTTING THINGS OFF*

Sadie would have been much happier when she headed home on Monday if she had listened to Mrs. Bertelli.

1. Look up *listen* in the dictionary and write out the meaning. Refer to James 1:19 in this week's WORDS TO LIVE BY.

2. How does God's Word counsel you to listen?

DAY FIVE: *LIVE IT!*

There was a time for Sadie to do homework and a time to spend with friends, but Sadie's priorities were askew.

Today, create a schedule for the afternoons in your week, making designated time for devotions, chores, games, homework, etc. Write it neatly on a clean sheet of paper and then hang it in your room as a reminder to manage your time wisely!

PRAYER

Heavenly Father,

Help me to manage my time wisely and to keep my priorities straight.
Help me to remember that there is a time for everything!

In Jesus' Name,
Amen

SNEAKY CHANDLER

He who conceals his sins does not prosper, but whoever
confesses and renounces them finds mercy.
(Proverbs 28:13)

Chandler's best friend, Drew, had some really exciting news!

"I got the coolest new thing today! It's a new cell phone, the one with tons of cool games!" He held the phone up to Chandler. It had a big touch screen and was red with orange flames going up the sides.

Chandler smiled and said, "Awesome!" But a little green monster was starting to grow deep inside, and it got bigger and bigger during school as he stared at the phone inside Drew's desk. It was the coolest phone...in Chandler's favorite colors... and Drew said that the phone had tons of cool games.

When Drew was out of the room, Chandler made a sneaky move and snatched the phone out of Drew's desk. He put it in his pocket and hummed a nonchalant tune as Drew walked in, smiling at Chandler. Chandler smiled back, although he didn't really feel like smiling at the moment. He felt a little guilty about stealing Drew's phone.

When Chandler got home, Drew's phone rang. His ring tone was a funky rap song, which made Chandler want to keep it even more. Chandler looked at the caller ID and saw that it was Drew's mom, wanting to know where Drew was.

Two seconds later, the house phone rang. Chandler answered it. "Hello?"

"Hey, Chandler, it's me, Drew."

"Oh hi, Drew. How are you?"

"Not good. My phone is missing! Someone must have taken it at school." While Drew was talking, the cell phone rang again. "He Chandler, that's my ring tone. Why is the song playing?"

Chandler thought fast. "Oh...um...I turned on the radio and that's the song that came on."

"Alright, then. See ya later." Drew hung up.

What was I thinking? sighed Chandler as he hung up the phone. *Drew is my best friend, yet I stole his phone. Then, I lied to him. Will Drew ever trust me again?*

Chandler decided to go ahead and come clean. He picked up the phone and nervously dialed Drew. Chandler waited, not knowing how Drew would react, but confident he was doing what was right in God's eyes.

WORDS TO LIVE BY

He who conceals his sins does not prosper, but whoever confesses and renounces them finds mercy.
(Proverbs 28:13)

And as for you, brothers, never tire of doing what is right.
(2 Thessalonians 3:13)

If we confess our sins, he is faithful and just and will forgive us our sins and purify us from all unrighteousness.
(1 John 1:9)

For the word of the LORD is right and true;
he is faithful in all he does.
(Psalm 33:4)

"Therefore, my brothers, I want you to know that through Jesus the forgiveness of sins is proclaimed to you.
(Acts 13:38)

DAY ONE: READ *SNEAKY CHANDLER*

Chandler and Drew were best friends, but their friendship reached a crisis when Drew got a cool new cell phone. Chandler was filled with envy.

1. How did Chandler choose to deal with his envy?

2. Name a time that you were envious of something belonging to your best friend. How did you choose to deal with your envy?

DAY TWO: READ *SNEAKY CHANDLER*

When Chandler arrived home, he received a call from Drew. Then, in talking with his best friend, Chandler found it necessary to lie. Sneaky Chandler shows you sin is not dormant; one sin will lead to another.

1. Name a time that you concealed a sin, only to have that sin lead to another.

2. Memorize Proverbs 28:13.

LIVING OUT GOD'S WORD!

DAY THREE: READ *SNEAKY CHANDLER*

Chandler knew he could conceal his sin no longer. He picked up the phone and called Drew, confident he was doing was right in God's eyes.

1. Where must you look to find what is right in God's eyes? Refer to Psalms 33:4 in this week's WORDS TO LIVE BY.

2. It wasn't easy for Chandler to do the right thing, nor will it be always easy for you. Nevertheless, of what must you never get tired of doing? Refer to 2 Thessalonians 3:13 in this week's WORDS TO LIVE BY.

DAY FOUR: READ *SNEAKY CHANDLER*

Will Drew forgive Chandler? The story ends and we are left hanging! In contrast, when you sin against God, His Word never leaves you hanging.

1. What can you know for sure? Refer to 1 John 1:9 in this week's WORDS TO LIVE BY.

2. Through Whom does this forgiveness come? Refer to Acts 13:38 in this week's WORDS TO LIVE BY.

DAY FIVE: *LIVE IT!*

If you have ever stolen something from someone and they didn't find out, take some time to pray and ask God for forgiveness. If you've never done that, good for you! Pray and ask God to help give you the strength not to steal anything in the future.

PRAYER

Heavenly Father,

Help me to confess and renounce my sins, knowing that with You, I will find forgiveness and mercy.

In Jesus' Name,
Amen

LIVING OUT GOD'S WORD!

PATIENCE 16

Be patient with everyone.
(1 Thessalonians 5:14)

"Is there any mail for me?" Nick pounced on his mom as she came in holding the mail.

She sifted through the pile. "Here's your sports magazine."

Nick took the magazine from his mom and ran upstairs. He read about football players, a lacrosse league coming to town, a skateboarder who broke a world record, and all the other sports articles. Soon he came to an advertisement for a new mountain bike. It was the coolest bike Nick had ever seen! And it was on sale at the sporting goods store so Nick could buy it and his mom wouldn't have to pay a penny! He was sure his mom would be happy about that.

"MOM!" Nick ran down the stairs clutching the ad. "Look! It's a neat new mountain bike, and I have enough money to buy it! Plus, my birthday's coming up, and we're going camping and hiking and biking soon...Can we go buy it now? Please?"

His mom laughed. "Nick, you'll have to wait. You have camp this week and we need to go school shopping."

"Yes, ma'am," Nick sighed. But inside he was thinking: *Wait! The bikes might be all gone!*

A week later Nick was with his Mom and they passed by the sporting goods store. Nick spotted the shiny new bike in the window.

"Mom?" he said, gesturing to the bike.

"I have a doctor's appointment," she said. "Maybe afterward."

Nick wanted to groan and stomp his foot, but he remained silent.

When they drove by again the next day, the bike was still there. Mom parked the car and took Nick in.

"This young man has been waiting patiently for this new mountain bike," Mom smiled. "We'd like it, please."

The salesman smiled and took the bike off the shelf. "Here ya go," he said. Nick took out his wallet to pay, but Mom was quicker and handed the man her credit card. Nick was confused.

"Happy birthday, Nick," said Mom as they walked out of the store with the new bike!

LIVING OUT GOD'S WORD!

WORDS TO LIVE BY

Similarly, encourage the young men to be self-controlled.
(Titus 2:6)

And we urge you, brothers, warn those who are idle,
encourage the timid, help the weak,
be patient with everyone.
(1 Thessalonians 5:14)

But the fruit of the Spirit is love, joy, peace, patience,
kindness, goodness, faithfulness,
gentleness and self-control...
(Galatians 5:22-23)

DAY ONE: READ *PATIENCE*

Nick saw an advertisement in his sports magazine for the coolest mountain bike he had ever seen. He wanted to buy it right away but his mom said he would have to wait.

1. Why did Nick think his mom would let him buy the bike right away?

2. Name a time you wanted something and had the money to buy it, but your mom told you to wait. How did you respond?

DAY TWO: READ *PATIENCE*

A week later Nick saw the same bike in the sporting goods store. He pointed it out to his mom, but again Nick was told to wait.

1. How did Nick want to respond to his mother? How did he respond?

2. What characteristic was evident in Nick? Refer to Titus 2:6 in this week's WORDS TO LIVE BY.

DAY THREE: READ *PATIENCE*

Nick's mom was pleased that Nick had patiently waited for the bike. This pleasure was evident as she spoke with the salesman. Webster's defines patience as the will or ability to wait or endure without complaint.

1. How did Nick's mom reward her son's patience?

2. Memorize 1 Thessalonians 5:14.

DAY FOUR: READ *PATIENCE*

Think about where you go each day, what you do and the people you are around.

1. Where do you see your lack of patience most?

2. From whom does patience come? Refer to Galatians 5:22 in this week's WORDS TO LIVE BY.

DAY FIVE: *LIVE IT!*

Keep a journal for one week. At the end of each day list:
- How did I show patience?
- How did I fail to show patience?

PRAYER

Heavenly Father,

When my Mom or Dad tells me to wait, please help me to obey and not insist on having my own way. Thank You.

In Jesus' Name,
Amen

LIVING OUT GOD'S WORD!

TRUE CONTENTMENT 17

Be content with what you have.
(Hebrews 13:5)

Amy and Nick, siblings ages 12 and 10, were heading to the Richards' house one afternoon.

"Ally and I are just gonna hang out," Amy said.

"Danny and I will play basketball," said Nick. "We've gotta work on a secret play for our team."

"Well, whatever you do," said Mrs. Goodman, "be good."

Amy and Nick's mouths dropped open in amazement when they saw the Richards' house. It was huge!

And there were better things to do than just hang out or play basketball. Each child had a Wii. There were tons of secret hiding spots to play hide and seek. But that wasn't all! The Richards' had an air hockey table, a pool table and a ping-pong table in their basement.

When they had finished playing inside, Ally, Amy, Danny, and Nick went outside to jump on the trampoline and explore the creek.

"I wish we had a Wii," Amy remarked wistfully on the way home.

"I wish we had an air hockey table in our basement," Nick agreed. "That totally rocks!"

"And the ping-pong table!"

"And the trampoline!"

"Kids!" cried Mrs. Goodman. "You should be content with what you have. Don't you already have fun things?"

"Yeah, but the Richards' have better stuff," said Amy, looking out the window of the car. She saw a rusty blue station wagon parked by a gravel lot. Three girls were pretending to have a party, and the mom was trying and failing to clean up the car.

"Nick! Look at those kids!" cried Amy. "Their clothes are torn and dirty, and one of the little girls is holding a teddy bear with a ton of holes in it!"

The kids sat in silence for a few minutes, and then Amy spoke. "Our house seems like a mansion compared to what they have...pretty much nothing."

"Definitely," Nick agreed. "Mom's right. We should be content with what we have 'cause we're fortunate to have a house to live in."

"I've got an idea," Amy suggested, turning to her brother. "We should ask God to help us be content."

"Good thinking!" Mrs. Goodman beamed at her kids. "Amy, Nick, why don't you go ahead and pray?"

It wasn't easy, but with prayer, Amy and Nick began to be content with what they had over the next week. Nick was content with having a house with no basement like the Richards'. And when Amy complained that her recent birthday party wasn't as nearly as amazing as Ally's, she remembered that the little girls on the street didn't even have a friend to invite to their party! Amy and Nick learned true contentment comes from God alone!

LIVING OUT GOD'S WORD!

WORDS TO LIVE BY

I can do everything through him who gives me strength.
(Philippians 4:13)

Keep your lives free from the love of money and be content with what you have, because God has said, "Never will I leave you; never will I forsake you."
(Hebrews 13:5)

But godliness with contentment is great gain.
(1 Timothy 6:6)

DAY ONE: READ *TRUE CONTENTMENT*

Amy and Nick were excited about spending time with their friends. The siblings were awed when they arrived, saw the size of the house and all the fun things the Richard's had.

1. How did the siblings feel about their own things after spending time at the home of their friends?

2. Why does this attitude dishonor God? Refer to Hebrews 13:5 in this week's WORDS TO LIVE BY.

DAY TWO: READ *TRUE CONTENTMENT*

TRUE CONTENTMENT shows there are not only children who have much more than you; it points to those children who have less as well.

1. What did Amy and Nick see on the way home that made Amy realize her stuff was cool after all?

2. Nick compared his stuff with that of others to determine whether or not his things were cool. Do you do the same thing? Explain.

DAY THREE: READ *TRUE CONTENTMENT*

When Nick decided that he really did have cool stuff, he agreed to join his sister and pray for contentment.

1. What is the secret of being content in any and every situation? Refer to Philippians 4:13 in this week's WORDS TO LIVE BY.

2. Memorize Hebrews 13:5.

DAY FOUR: READ *TRUE CONTENTMENT*

Amy and Nick began to complain after playing at the home of friends whom they thought had better things.

1. List some things you have complained about this past week.

2. Think about the reason you complained. Was it because one or more of your friends had something that seemed better? Who decides what is better?

DAY FIVE: *LIVE IT!*

1. Take the list of complaints from DAY FOUR and pray specifically about each one over the next few days. Ask the Lord to help you be content.

2. Write out 1 Timothy 6:6.

PRAYER

Heavenly Father,

I'm sorry for the times I have complained to my mom and dad because they haven't given me everything I want. Please help me to be content with what I have.

In Jesus' Name,
Amen

_____

_____

_____

_____

_____

_____

_____

_____

_____

_____

_____

_____

_____

_____

_____

_____

_____

_____

STAY AWAY! 18

A wise son heeds his father's instruction, but a mocker
does not listen to rebuke.
(Proverbs 13:1)

One sunny day, Nick and his older sister, Amy, were walking to the park to feed the ducks.

"Let's take a shortcut," Nick suggested, and turned onto Beacon Street—a seldom used side street.

However, Beacon Street was scary. Mean dogs barked as Nick and Amy walked down the street. Houses were falling apart. Trash was everywhere, and graffiti was on almost every building.

Nick and Amy got to the park, fed the ducks, and walked home without using Beacon Street. When they got home, they immediately called their dad, who was at work.

"Stay away from Beacon Street from now on," he instructed. "That area is dangerous, especially at night, and I don't want anything to happen to you."

Amy listened dutifully, but Nick rolled his eyes. He was ten. Nothing could happen to him!

The next Saturday, Nick and his friends, Santiago and Darien, were going to the sports store to get some baseball gear. On the way, they passed Beacon Street. "Hey, I dare you to walk down that street," Santiago dared Nick.

"OK," Nick agreed, Dad's words never coming to mind. Halfway down the street, a pit bull started to chase him. Nick hollered and started to run. Unfortunately, the pit bull bit his leg, and the next thing he knew, Nick was in the hospital with an IV tube hooked up to his arm. He hurt so much and felt awful.

"Nick, you should have listened to me," Dad chided. "I told you to stay away from Beacon Street for a reason. That dog was rabid! I'm so thankful you're OK—that was a bad bite."

Nick agreed. He should have listened to Dad. Next time, he would listen and obey his father.

LIVING OUT GOD'S WORD!

WORDS TO LIVE BY

A wise son heeds his father's instruction, but a mocker does not listen to rebuke.

(Proverbs 13:1)

When pride comes, then comes disgrace, but with humility comes wisdom.

(Proverbs 11:2)

But the wisdom that comes from heaven is first of all pure; then peace-loving, considerate, submissive, full of mercy and good fruit, impartial and sincere.

(James 3:17)

DAY ONE: READ *STAY AWAY!*

When Nick and Amy called their dad after returning from the park, they told him about their time on Beacon Street.

1. What were the two reasons Nick's dad gave for staying away from Beacon Street?

2. When a parent warns you of the danger of something, do you believe it is for your own good? Why or why not?

DAY TWO: READ *STAY AWAY!*

The instruction you receive from a parent or teacher will not benefit you at all unless you take it to heart.

1. Why did Nick ignore his father's instructions about Beacon Street?

2. Name a time that you responded to one of your parents in the same way. What happened as a result of your attitude?

DAY THREE: READ *STAY AWAY!*

Nick did not realize the importance of taking his father's instruction to heart until it was too late.

1. List the order of events that led Nick to admit that he should have listened to his dad.

2. Memorize Proverbs 13:1.

DAY FOUR: READ *STAY AWAY!*

Nick's pride caused him to dismiss his father's instruction. Therefore, when Santiago dared him to walk down Beacon Street, the words of Nick's dad never came to mind.

1. The opposite of pride is humility. Look up humility in the dictionary and write out the meaning.

2. What comes with humility? Refer to Proverbs 11:2 in this week's WORDS TO LIVE BY.

DAY FIVE: *LIVE IT!*

The wisdom that comes from heaven comes from God. Therefore, a wise son or daughter in God's eyes is one whose source of wisdom is the Word of God.

1. Read James 3:17. List the eight qualities of heavenly wisdom mentioned in this verse.

2. In the next few days, look for opportunities to show God's wisdom in one of these ways.

PRAYER

Heavenly Father,

Forgive me for the times that I have followed the example of Nick and blew off the instructions of my parents.

Help me to grasp the importance of heeding their instruction, for this is heavenly wisdom.

In Jesus' Name,
Amen

LIVING OUT GOD'S WORD!

_____

_____

_____

_____

_____

_____

_____

_____

_____

_____

_____

_____

_____

_____

_____

_____

THE CANDY STORE

Children, obey your parents in the LORD,
for this is right...
(Ephesians 6:1)

Sadie, Virginia, and Grace stood outside of the candy store on Porter Street.

"Oh come on, Sadie," Grace was saying. "You can have candy. Don't worry that your dad says you can't have candy because it causes cavities."

"Yeah, Sadie, whatever," Virginia exclaimed. "I eat candy—like, every day and don't get any cavities."

Deep down in Sadie's gut, she knew it was wrong to disobey her parents. But she let her friends drag her into the candy store and make her buy licorice whips.

Later, at home, Dad asked her about her black tongue.

"Oh, that," Sadie tried to appear unconcerned. "It was some mint I chewed. It just turned my tongue black." *There. That wasn't so bad. A little white lie never hurts anybody,* Sadie thought.

Mom asked her at supper.

"Uh, I chewed a mint that made my tongue turn black. It tasted really gross!"

Her parents looked at each other strangely.

Sadie's sister looked at her that night. "Whoa, girl, your breath smells like that Twizzler licorice stuff Virginia and Grace eat. What's wrong?"

Sadie knew she couldn't hold the truth in any longer. She poured the whole story out.

"I let Virginia and Grace buy me some licorice whips at the candy store. I ate it, even though I knew it was wrong, and then lied to Mom and Dad about it."

Later, Sadie confessed to her parents the whole truth.

"Sadie, you disobeyed us and lied," Dad explained to a tearful Sadie. "You need to apologize to your mom and I, and I think you need to let Grace and Virginia stop trying to take advantage of you."

"I'm so, so, sorry, Dad," Sadie cried. "I sinned. Will you forgive me?"

As Sadie hugged her parents, she thought, *Well, even though a white lie might cover it up, it hurts you in the end.*

WORDS TO LIVE BY

*Anyone, then, who knows the good he ought to do and
doesn't do it, sins.*

(James 4:17)

ALIVE IN HIM!

DAY ONE: READ *THE CANDY STORE*

Virginia, Grace, and Sadie stopped at the candy store one day, but Sadie's dad had instructed her to not buy candy, because it was bad for her teeth.

1. What did Virginia and Grace say which showed their lack of respect for the authority of Sadie's parents?

2. Name a time you were asked to ignore the instruction of your parents. Explain.

DAY TWO: READ *THE CANDY STORE*

Sadie was faced with the choice of obeying her dad or following her peers.

1. What did Sadie choose to do?

2. Can you relate to Sadie's decision to please her peers, rather than her parents? If so, how?

LIVING OUT GOD'S WORD!

DAY THREE: READ *THE CANDY STORE*

Sadie's lied to her parents when they asked why her teeth were black and they appeared to believe her. Later, however, when Sadie's sister confronted her, Sadie told her the truth. Her sister encouraged Sadie to tell their mom and dad what she had done.

1. How did Sadie respond to the advice of her sister?

2. Name a time when a sibling caught you in a lie.

3. Did you listen when he/she encouraged you to tell your parents the truth?

4. If not, why not?

DAY FOUR: READ *THE CANDY STORE*

Sadie knew it was wrong to listen to Virginia and Grace, but she did it anyhow.

1. What does God call what Sadie did? Refer to James 4:17 in this week's WORDS TO LIVE BY.

2. Memorize James 4:17.

DAY FIVE: *LIVE IT!*

Think back on this week. Did you do something or go somewhere with a group of friends where they persuaded you to do something that you have been told not to do? What was it? Name all the times if more than one. What was the outcome? Did your parents ever find out? If so, how were you disciplined?

PRAYER

Heavenly Father,

Forgive me for the times I have willfully sinned against you by listening to my friends instead of my parents. When I face the choice to obey my parents or please my friends, help me to do what is right in your eyes.

In Jesus' Name,
Amen

LIVING OUT GOD'S WORD!

_____

_____

_____

_____

_____

_____

_____

_____

_____

_____

_____

_____

_____

_____

_____

_____

_____

_____

_____

NOBLE AND RIGHT?

Finally, brothers, whatever is true, whatever is noble,
whatever is right, whatever is pure, whatever is lovely,
whatever is admirable—if anything is
excellent or praiseworthy—
think about such things.
(Philippians 4:8)

Drew and his sister, Della, had a whole week off for spring break, and they were just staying home, which made Drew doubly happy. He could sleep in and watch all the TV he wanted.

The first day of spring break, Drew was up in his room watching cartoons when an advertisement came on for a new TV show on channel 13. It looked really cool, so the next day, Drew got up early to watch it.

But he realized that it wasn't as mild as it looked: the characters used swear words and used God's name in vain, plus there was plenty of violence and sword fights. Drew just kept on watching the show, every single morning of break. Even after break ended, he'd get up early to watch the show.

Two weeks after spring break, Drew got his science test back. Drew took one look at his grade—a C minus—and uttered a swear word he had heard the main character use. The word happened to be one of the worst swear words, and his table mates, Chandler and Nick, heard him say it. Unfortunately, the teacher, Mr. Naylor, also heard it.

"Drew," Mr. Naylor addressed him sternly, "I would like to see you in the hall, please."

Drew gulped as he shuffled dejectedly out into the hall, Mr. Naylor behind him.

"Drew," Mr. Naylor said, "I am extremely disappointed in you. You said a bad word and set a bad example for your classmates. I'm sorry, Drew, but I must send you to Principal Kennedy's office."

As Mr. Naylor wrote out a note, Drew felt so upset inside. He would stop watching that show and would try to stay away from any other inappropriate television shows. He would also try to keep his mind away from bad things and do something more fun in the future, like play baseball with Nick or practice the trumpet. Next time, he would think on the right things.

LIVING OUT GOD'S WORD!

WORDS TO LIVE BY

For the word of the LORD is right and true;
he is faithful in all he does.

(Psalm 33:4)

Finally, brothers, whatever is true, whatever is noble,
whatever is right, whatever is pure, whatever is lovely,
whatever is admirable—if anything is excellent or praise-
worthy—think about such things.

(Philippians 4:8)

ALIVE IN HIM!

DAY ONE: READ *NOBLE AND RIGHT?*

During spring break Drew began watching a television show filled with violence and bad language.

1. When did the influence of this show become apparent?

2. Think about the television shows you are watching. What effect are they having on you? Are they influencing the way you talk, dress, or behave?

DAY TWO: READ *NOBLE AND RIGHT?*

Drew's bad language did not escape the ears of his teacher and he was sent to the principal's office.

1. How did Drew respond?

2. Name a time that you were disciplined at school or at home. How did you respond?

DAY THREE: READ *NOBLE AND RIGHT?*

The discipline Drew received at school was meant for his good, to correct his bad behavior.

1. What kind of example was Drew setting for his class-mates when he used bad language?

2. Think about the way you talk and act around your classmates? What kind of example are you?

DAY FOUR: READ *NOBLE AND RIGHT?*

After he was disciplined at school, Drew decided to change and do what was right.

1. Where do you find what is right? Refer to Psalm 33:4 in this week's WORDS TO LIVE BY.

2. Memorize Philippians 4:8.

DAY FIVE: *LIVE IT!*

On DAY ONE you were asked to think about how the television shows you were watching influenced you. Make a list of the television shows you watch on a regular basis. When you watch them over this next week, think about what you are watching. Do the characters in the show speak and act in line with God's Word? If not, pray and ask the Lord to give you something better to do at that time.

PRAYER

Heavenly Father,

You tell us, whatever is true, whatever is noble, whatever is right, whatever is pure, whatever is lovely, whatever is admirable—if anything is excellent or praiseworthy— think about such things. Will you help me to obey this command?

In Jesus' Name,
Amen

LIVING OUT GOD'S WORD!

_____

_____

_____

_____

_____

_____

_____

_____

_____

_____

_____

_____

_____

_____

_____

_____

_____

_____

WINNER'S PRIDE

Let another praise you and not your own mouth; someone else and not your own lips.
(Proverbs 27:2)

"Dad! Dad! Guess what?"

Drew's dad stepped out on the front porch to see Drew and Della running home from the bus stop, backpacks bouncing, smiles a mile wide on their faces.

"Hello, Della," He hugged his youngest child. "What's up, Drew?" he asked his oldest.

"Guess what?" Drew responded. "I won first place in the writing contest!"

"That's awesome!" Dad high-fived Drew.

"Can I ride my bike to the park?" Drew asked. "It's Friday...and I won the writing contest!"

Dad laughed. "Go ahead," he said. "Have fun, stay safe, and make sure the ducks don't chase after Della." Della always went with Drew to the park.

When Drew and Della arrived at Abernathy Park, Della went to play on the playground and Drew headed over to the basketball court, immediately spotting Chandler, Nick, and Alison, his friends from school.

"Hey, guess what?" Drew said. "I won first place in the writing contest!"

"Cool!" said Alison as they quickly formed teams.

The game was fun and well played, but Drew could only talk about his recent win. "I get to move on to the state contest, and if I win, I get an iPod and a hundred dollars!" Drew went on and on about his win.

Suddenly, Drew spotted Alison, Nick, and Chandler walking away. "Hey, you guys!" Drew called, starting to run after them. "Wait!"

The three turned around as Drew reached them, panting heavily. "Where are you goin'?"

"Home," Nick responded firmly.

"Why?" Drew pressed.

"Dude, you were bragging the whole time about winning. It makes us feel bad that we didn't win. Plus, you spoiled the game. It's no fun listening to you brag." Chandler said, and the three whirled around.

"Wait!" Drew sighed, but they kept walking. *I shouldn't have bragged about winning, he sighed. Then I might have been able to play longer.*

LIVING OUT GOD'S WORD!

WORDS TO LIVE BY

For by the grace given me I say to every one of you: Do not think of yourself more highly than you ought, but rather think of yourself with sober judgment, in accordance with the measure of faith God has given you.

(Romans 12:3)

Let another praise you, and not your own mouth; someone else, and not your own lips.

(Proverbs 27:2)

Pride only breeds quarrels,
but wisdom is found in those who take advice.

(Proverbs 13:10a)

ALIVE IN HIM!

DAY ONE: READ *WINNER'S PRIDE*

After telling his dad he won the writing contest, Drew rode his bike to the park. There he met Chandler, Nick and Alison and they formed teams for a game of basketball.

1. What did Drew talk about the whole time he was playing?

2. Name a time you were honored for something. The honor may be from your school, your home or your church. Is that all you could talk about? Explain.

DAY TWO: READ *WINNER'S PRIDE*

Drew's dad and Alison had both acknowledged Drew's honor, but that did not satisfy Drew's pride. He wanted to be the center of attention.

1. How did Drew's friends react to his proud attitude?

2. What was Drew doing that God said we should not do? Refer to Romans 12:3 in this week's WORDS TO LIVE BY.

DAY THREE: READ *WINNER'S PRIDE*

Drew arrived at the park full of pride, but left filled with regrets.

1. What might have happened if Drew had focused on the game instead of himself?

2. Memorize Proverbs 27:2.

DAY FOUR: READ *WINNER'S PRIDE*

Drew's pursuit of Chandler, Nick and Alison shows he was not aware that he had offended them. Drew was blind to his pride, but his eyes were opened when his teammates left feeling hurt and angry.

1. What does pride do? Refer to Proverbs 13:10 in this week's WORDS TO LIVE BY.

2. Name a time one of your peers fussed at you. Was your pride the reason? Why or why not?

DAY FIVE: *LIVE IT!*

Keep a journal over the next five days. At the end of each day, reflect on the conversations that you had with friends and family. Did you try to dominate? Or did you listen and show an interest in others?

PRAYER

Heavenly Father,

Forgive me for the times I have allowed my pride to cause a falling out with my friends or family. When I am tempted to boast or brag about what I've done, please help me to obey your Word and let another praise me and not my own lips.

In Jesus' Name,
Amen

LIVING OUT GOD'S WORD!

_____

_____

_____

_____

_____

_____

_____

_____

_____

_____

_____

_____

_____

_____

_____

_____

THE BROKEN VASE

*Keep your tongue from speaking evil
and your lips from speaking lies.*
(Psalm 34:13)

Chandler was home alone one day while Mom was shopping, so he decided to kick the soccer ball around the living room. It got boring fast, so he decided to give the ball one powerful kick. The ball bounced off the ceiling, zinged off the coffee table, flew through the air, and decided it wanted to crash into Mom's thousand-dollar vase. The vase shattered into a million pieces, and the ball slowly rolled to a stop at Chandler's feet.

Chandler smacked the side of his head. "Aw, darn it!" he cried. "Mom's going to be so mad at me." He did his best to sweep up the pieces, but there were too many. Finally, he gave up and settled down for a nap on the couch.

Chandler was awakened twenty minutes later by Mom. "Chandler, why on earth is my best vase broken?"

Thankfully, Chandler had put the ball into the garage after the vase was wrecked. "Uh, well, I opened the window to let in some fresh air. A bird flew in and sat on the vase, and Tramp spotted it," Chandler gestured to the slobbering bulldog laying on the kitchen floor. "And you know Tramp! He leapt up to get the bird and knocked over the vase. I chased the bird back out and shut the window." He added a nervous laugh. There. That wasn't so bad! It was just a little white lie. Chandler thought.

Mom bought it. "Let's see if Dad can fix it." she said.

An hour later, Dad was examining the vase. "Huh. This vase may be able to be fixed, but I doubt it." He stood up and glanced at Chandler. "What happened?"

"Well, I opened the window to let in some fresh air, and a bird flew in. Tramp heard the chirping and started to bark. The bird was terrified and started flying around in circles. Tramp chased the bird around the room until it landed on the vase. Tramp leapt for the vase and knocked it over." Chandler smiled nervously. "I chased the bird back out, closed the window, and settled Tramp in his cage."

"Wait a second," Mom said, confused. "I thought the bird sat on the vase, and didn't fly around."

"And why is Tramp over there on the armchair when he was supposed to be in his cage?" Dad asked suspiciously.

"Well..." Chandler laughed nervously, staring uncomfortably at his parents.

Then it clicked. "Chandler! Are you lying to us?" Mom demanded, one eyebrow arched.

Chandler stuttered, "I...I...ok. I broke the vase 'cause I was kicking the ball around." he sighed.

Drew's dad sighed heavily. "Chandler, if you had been honest with us in the first place, you wouldn't have gotten in as much trouble. However, since you lied to both your mom and I, you're grounded for two weeks."

"But what about the football clinic I was gonna sign up for?" cried Chandler, very close to breaking into tears.

"You're grounded," Mom repeated sternly. "I'm sorry, Chandler. I don't want to do this, but sin has its consequences."

Chandler blinked back tears as he nodded slowly. Lying had seemed harmless at the time, but it turned out to be harmful.

LIVING OUT GOD'S WORD!

WORDS TO LIVE BY

*Keep your tongue from evil and your lips
from speaking lies.*
(Psalm 34:13)

*There are six things the LORD hates, seven that are detest-
able to him: haughty eyes, a lying tongue,
hands that shed innocent blood.*
(Proverbs 6:16-17)

DAY ONE: READ *THE BROKEN VASE*

While kicking the soccer ball around the living room, Chandler broke an expensive vase belonging to his mom.

1. What did Chandler tell his mom when she asked him about the broken vase?

2. Can you relate to Chandler in any way? In what way?

DAY TWO: READ *THE BROKEN VASE*

Chandler made up a story, blaming their dog for knocking over the vase. He knew he was lying, but excused his behavior by thinking, *It was just a little white lie.*

1. What does God's Word say about lying? Refer to Psalm 34:13 and Proverbs 6:16-17 in this week's WORDS TO LIVE BY.

2. Are there little white lies? Why or why not?

DAY THREE: READ *THE BROKEN VASE*

Chandler thought his mother had bought his lie, but he was wrong. When his dad questioned him, Chandler's story changed and his parents knew he had lied to them.

1. Why is it more difficult to keep telling a lie than to tell the truth?

2. Name a time you tried to hide what really happened by telling a lie. What was the result?

DAY FOUR: READ *THE BROKEN VASE*

The story of THE BROKEN VASE shows the foolishness of trying to hide the truth behind a lie.

1. What lesson did Chandler learn when he was grounded for two weeks?

2. Memorize Psalm 34:13.

DAY FIVE: *LIVE IT!*

Think back about your week. Did you lie? Did you ever change the truth only a little bit in order to stay out of trouble? (Changing the truth even a little is still a lie!) Write down your answers, then pray and ask God for forgiveness.

PRAYER

Heavenly Father,

Forgive me for the times I've lied and, like Chandler, justifying my behavior. When I am tempted to lie, please help me to remember to keep my tongue from evil and my lips from speaking lies.

In Jesus' Name,
Amen

_____

_____

_____

_____

_____

_____

_____

_____

_____

_____

_____

_____

_____

_____

_____

_____

A TRUE FRIEND?

A righteous man is cautious in friendships.
(Proverbs 12:26a)

Grace was looking for someone to sit with at lunch one day. Her old friend, Tanya, had moved away, and now, Grace was looking for a new friend. The only girls' table with an open spot was the table belonging to Trish, Cameron, and Christy. Grace shyly approached the girls and said, "Can I sit here?"

Trish smiled. "Sure! Sit down!" she exclaimed. "Oh, hi, Grace, it's you! I didn't recognize you at first." Cameron and Christy giggled. Trish giggled a little too, then turned to Grace. "We were just planning to go to the mall Saturday. Do you wanna come?"

"Sure," Grace said. "Ever since Tanya moved, I've been looking for someone to hang out with."

Christy shot Trish a look, but Trish paid no attention. "Oh yeah, Tanya," she said. "Yeah, you guys did hang out a lot."

The bell rang and lunch was over. As the girls got up, Trish said, "Bring some change on Saturday. Tell your mom that my dad will pick you up!" As Grace nodded and walked back to class, she smiled. Her parents would love it that Grace had found a new friend! And sure enough, her mom was very happy when she found that Grace was going to hang out with the girls.

The next day, Grace found Trish before class. "My mom says it's OK for me to go with you guys to the mall on Saturday."

Trish turned to Grace with her green eyes as cold as ice. "What are you talking about, Grace? I sure didn't invite you to come to the mall with us. And if I did, then it was a mistake. We'd never hang out with you." Trish turned back to Cameron and Christy. She whispered something to them, and then they all laughed loudly and rudely. Cameron turned to Grace with a smirk on her face and continued to laugh.

Grace walked away. She was hopping that she and Trish could be friends. She was so upset that Trish had done that to her. Why? Grace was so confused.

WORDS TO LIVE BY

A righteous man is cautious in friendship...
(Proverbs 12:26a)

*A friend loves at all times, and a brother is born
for adversity.*
(Proverbs 17:17)

*Love must be sincere. Hate what is evil;
cling to what is good.*
(Romans 12:9)

ALIVE IN HIM!

DAY ONE: READ *A TRUE FRIEND?*

Grace, wanting a friend, approached some girls in the lunchroom and asked if she could join them.

1. Where did one of the girls invite Grace to go?

2. Can you relate to Grace's desire for a friend and her excitement about the invitation she received? In what way?

DAY TWO: READ *A TRUE FRIEND?*

Grace's mom was happy her daughter found some friends and gave her permission to go to the mall. But Grace's excitement was soon extinguished.

1. How did Trish respond when Grace told her she could go to the mall?

2. Have you ever been invited to go somewhere and then found you were not really wanted? If so, explain.

DAY THREE: READ *A TRUE FRIEND?*

The giggles and the looks that took place at the table showed that Trish and her friends were not really interested in hanging out with Grace. But Grace didn't notice.

1. About what does God's Word tell you be cautious? Refer to Proverbs 12:26a in this week's WORDS TO LIVE BY.

2. Do you have a friend like Trish who treats you differently, depending on the situation or who is around?

DAY FOUR: READ *A TRUE FRIEND?*

The story A TRUE FRIEND shows the importance of caution in friendship.

1. What does God Word say about friends? Refer to Proverbs 17:17 in this week's WORDS TO LIVE BY.

2. What kind of love does God require? Refer to Romans 12:9 and Proverbs 6:16-17 in this week's WORDS TO LIVE BY.

DAY FIVE: *LIVE IT!*

Memorize Proverbs 12:26a.

Grace thought she made a new friend, but she was wrong. Trish was not the friend Grace had hoped for. Confused and upset, she walked away. Now, list the names of your closest friends. Next to each name, write the reason or reasons you have chosen that particular friend. Review the list. Based on what you've learned this week, are there any friendships from which you must walk away?

PRAYER

Heavenly Father,

Thank you for the friends you have given me. Help me to be cautious when I change schools or when a friend moves away and I must look for new friends.

In Jesus' Name,
Amen

TALE OF THE NOT SO IDENTICAL TWINS 24

The LORD guides the humble in what is right and teaches
them his way.
(Psalm 25:9)

Alison and Alena Patterson were twins. They looked exactly alike: curly blond hair, freckles, green eyes, and the little birthmark shaped like an oval by their right ear. But their habits and personalities were different.

Alison was studious, polite, and helpful; while Alena didn't do well in school, forgot her manners, and didn't help when others needed her to.

"Alison!" Dad called one night. "Go tell your sister it's time to eat and then come down to the kitchen!"

Alison walked to Alena's room. "Time to eat, Alena," Alison said. "C'mon."

Alena tossed her head. "I'm painting my nails, Alison, can't you see that?" she said in a superior tone. "I'll be down when I've finished putting glitter on them."

Alison sighed and went to the kitchen, where a hot supper was waiting, along with Mom and Dad. "Where's Alena?" Mom asked.

"She wouldn't come," Alison said, putting her napkin in her lap.

"ALENA!" Dad yelled. "Come on, sweetie!" The family prayed and began to eat. Alena came down ten minutes later with green, glittery fingernails.

Alena sat down and started wolfing down her food, unlike Alison, who was chewing one bite at a time.

"Alena," said Mom painfully. "Please, put your napkin in your lap and eat like a lady. We've told you to do so many times."

"Ummhmm," Alena chewed, and then obeyed.

After dinner, Alison got out her papers to study for a science test. "Alena, come study with me, please," she urged.

"No way," Alena said. "I'm not studying. I can make an A without opening a book," she bragged. She went off to go e-mail her friends.

But the next day, Alison came home with an A on her test and Alena came home with a C. "Oh well," Alena sighed remorsefully. "Let's go ride our scooters."

They got their scooters and their helmets out. Alison put hers on, but Alena tossed hers aside. Alison tried to warn her, but Alena was already on the road.

When a car came speeding down the street, Alison moved aside, but Alena waited until the last minute and flung herself onto the curb. Alena hit her head badly and had a concussion.

One day later, Alena lay in her hospital bed and sighed, *Why haven't I been doing the right thing?*

LIVING OUT GOD'S WORD!

WORDS TO LIVE BY

Be completely humble and gentle; be patient, bearing with one another in love.

(Ephesians 4:2)

Take my yoke upon you and learn from me,
for I am gentle and humble in heart,
and you will find rest for your souls.

(Matthew 11:29)

He guides the humble in what is right and
teaches them his way.

(Psalm 25:9)

DAY ONE: READ
TALE OF THE NOT SO
IDENTICAL TWINS

Alena was Alison's twin sister, but was completely oppo-site of her in her attitude and actions.

1. What words could characterize Alena?

2. Do you relate to Alena in any way? If so, how?

DAY TWO: READ
TALE OF THE NOT SO
IDENTICAL TWINS

1. What words could characterize Alison?

2. Do you relate to Alison in any way? If so, how?

DAY THREE: READ
TALE OF THE NOT SO
IDENTICAL TWINS

The *TALE OF THE NOT SO IDENTICAL TWINS* ends with Alena in a hospital bed suffering from a head injury. She was filled with regrets over her action, but until Alena repents of her pride, she'll continue behaving foolishly.

1. The opposite of pride is humility. What does God's Word command you to be? Refer to Ephesians4:2 in this week's WORDS TO LIVE BY.

2. To whom must you go to learn how to live out this command? Refer to Matthew 11:29 in this week's WORDS TO LIVE BY.

DAY FOUR: READ
TALE OF THE NOT SO
IDENTICAL TWINS

Alena's haughty attitude was evident in the way she responded to her parents, her sister, her studies and safety rules.

1. Who does the LORD guide in what is right? Refer to Psalm 25:9 in this week's WORDS TO LIVE BY.

2. Memorize Psalm 25:9.

DAY FIVE: *LIVE IT!*

Begin each morning of this coming week with the following prayer:

Heavenly Father,

Please guide me in what is right and teach me your way.

In Jesus' Name,
Amen

At the end of the week, list the ways the Lord guided you to do what is right in His eyes.

PRAYER

Heavenly Father,

Thank you for being my guide and teacher. Please help me to live each day for you.

In Jesus' Name,
Amen

LIVING OUT GOD'S WORD!

SPORTS KID

Love the Lord your God with all your heart and with all your soul and with all your mind.
(Matthew 22:37)

Drew biked down Lambert Road quickly. Today, he had football practice, and he couldn't wait to be there.

"Hey, Drew!" Drew's best friend, Nick called from his front porch. "Whatcha doin'?"

"Going to football practice," Drew said. "I gotta tell everyone about this big play I thought up!" He sped away.

On Tuesday, Chandler called Drew on his cell phone. "Hi, Drew," Chandler said. "Are you signed up for VBS next week? You really should come!"

"Nah. Why?" Drew asked, doodling soccer balls on a page.

"I need to bring a friend with me. C'mon, it'll be fun!"

"No way! I've got to watch this hockey tournament next week. It's the post-season, and I have to know who wins."

"Oh. Well, goodbye."

Thursday, while Drew was playing basketball in the backyard, his mom came outside.

"Drew," she called. "Time for Bible club. You've got verses you need to say to Miss Snow, and you haven't been there for two weeks," she said, wiping her hands on her jeans.

Drew bounced the ball and walked over to her, wiping the sweat from his forehead. "Can I skip this one? I'm playing basketball." His mom reluctantly agreed.

On Saturday, Chandler, Nick, and a few other boys were at the park playing volleyball. Drew was riding his bike on one of the trails when they saw him.

"Hi, Drew," Nick wiped perspiration off his red cheeks. Chandler waved. "Didn't see you at Bible club on Thursday. Which reminds me—are you going to the Sunday school picnic tomorrow?"

"Chips, soda, candy...food heaven!" Chandler exclaimed.

"Are you kidding? I've got a football game tomorrow," Drew said. "I don't want to miss it!" He quickly pedaled off.

Early Sunday morning, Drew's mom came into his room. Drew groaned as she turned on the light.

"Drew," she said, "you've missed three weeks of Bible Club and a week of church. You need to go today."

"But I was planning to play the multi-player football tournament online this morning!"

"Church is more important than any of your activities," Mom said as she left the room.

Drew sighed. As he started to think about his actions over the past couple of weeks and what Mom had said to him, he realized that Mom was right, and that he had not been putting God first in his life. He sighed guiltily, and started to pray and ask God for forgiveness. After he finished, he felt much better knowing that from now on, God would be finishing in first place.

WORDS TO LIVE BY

See to it, brothers, that none of you has a sinful, unbeliev-
ing heart that turns away from the living God.
(Hebrews 3:12)

Jesus replied: "Love the Lord your God with all your heart
and with all your soul and with all your This is the first and
greatest commandment.
(Matthew 22:37-38)

DAY ONE: READ *SPORTS KID*

Drew attended Bible Club and church, but he stopped going to them when his love for sports became the focus of his life.

1. How did Drew respond when his friends encouraged him to join them in church related activities?

2. Have you lost interest in attending church or in church related activities? If so, what has taken its place?

DAY TWO: READ *SPORTS KID*

Drew's mom reluctantly agreed to let Drew play basketball instead of going to Bible Club, but insisted he attend church.

1. What did Drew realize when his mom told him that church was more important than any of his other activities?

2. When you, like Drew, put sports, hobbies, or anything else you enjoy as the focus of your life, who are you turning away from? Refer to Hebrews 3:12 in this week's WORDS TO LIVE BY.

DAY THREE: READ *SPORTS KID*

SPORTS KID shows how friends differ when it comes to the priority they place on activities that reflect their relationship with Jesus Christ.

1. Can you relate to Drew's attitude toward church? If so, explain.

2. Can you relate to the way Drew's friends Nick and Chandler encouraged him? If so, how?

DAY FOUR: READ *SPORTS KID*

Nick and Chandler enjoyed sports, but unlike Drew, they did not make sports the focus of their lives, allowing it to control everything he did.

1. Chandler and Nick enjoyed sports, but unlike Drew, they did not make sports the focus of their lives. Refer to Matthew 22:37-38in this week's WORDS TO LIVE BY.

2. Memorize Matthew 22:37-38.

DAY FIVE: *LIVE IT!*

List all your activities this week. Are any of these taking the place of activities focusing on God? If so, why do you choose these activities over activities involving church and God's Word? Do your activities and attitudes show a love for God or for yourself?

PRAYER

Heavenly Father,

Thank You for showing how much You love me by sending Your Son to die on the cross for my sins. Help me to love You with all my heart and all my soul and all my mind.

> *In Jesus' Name,*
> *Amen*

LIVING OUT GOD'S WORD!

YOU ARE LOVED 26

Give thanks to the LORD, for he is good.
His love endures forever.
(Psalm 136:1)

Nick sighed as he got off the bus from middle school one warm, sunny March afternoon. Absolutely nothing had gone right at school! First, he sang a C sharp three times instead of a C during chorus, making the whole tenor section mess up. Then, he was tripped in the middle of the hallway on the way to lunch and the whole class laughed at him. He had made a failing grade on a math project and one of his best friends was spreading rumors about him. He felt like an outcast!

Dad was making guacamole when Nick entered the back door in the kitchen. "Hey, Nick, what's up?" He fist-bumped his son.

"Nothin' much," Nick sighed, and immediately, Dad sensed something wasn't right in Nick's world. "Got some math to finish up for homework."

"Mom's going to be home soon from work if you need to talk," Dad said gently.

Nick's brown eyes filled with tears as he was reminded of the bad day. He rubbed them away with one angry swipe and headed upstairs.

Nick was trying to figure out how to find the area of a circle for his homework when someone knocked on his door. "Can I come in?" It was Mom, home from work.

"Yeah, I guess," Nick shrugged.

Mom came in and shut the door behind her. She was still dressed in her skirt, blazer, and blouse from her job at the bank. "So. Dad tells me that things weren't the best for you at school today?" She kicked off her high heels.

"Uh-huh," Nick nodded; lower lip quivering, and the tears finally spilled over as he opened up to Mom about the day—and his problems at school. Nick often had to stop to think or let out a big wail, and Mom listened carefully.

She patted Nick's back as he gulped in big breaths of air. "Son, look at me." Mom said.

Nick turned and did so.

"Nick," Mom said. "I know you want your peers to always like you and treat you well, but some days they will like you and some days they won't. And you may, or may not, know the reason.

"But listen carefully! One thing will never change! God loves you and His love endures forever. Don't ever forget this!"

Mom gave Nick's shoulders a squeeze. "I have to go pick your sister up from lacrosse now. I love you!"

"I love you too, Mom. Thanks for talking with me," Nick called as she left and closed the door behind her. He even smiled as he resumed his homework!

LIVING OUT GOD'S WORD!

WORDS TO LIVE BY

For I am convinced that neither death nor life, neither angels nor demons, neither the present nor the future, nor any powers, neither height nor depth, nor anything else in all creation, will be able to separate us from the love of God that is in Christ Jesus our Lord.

(Romans 8:38-39)

Your love, O LORD, reaches to the heavens, your faithfulness to the skies.

(Psalm 36:5)

Give thanks to the LORD, for he is good. His love endures forever.

(Psalm 136:1)

DAY ONE: READ *YOU ARE LOVED*

Nick was not feeling good about himself for some time.

1. What happened at school that discouraged Nick even further?

2. Do you relate to Nick in any way? If so, how?

DAY TWO: READ *YOU ARE LOVED*

Nick's dad sensed his son needed to talk, but felt Nick's mom was the one to handle the situation. Nick's mom listened carefully as Nick opened up to her about his day.

1. To whom and what did his mom first direct Nick's attention?

2. How far does God's love reach? Refer to Psalm 36:5 in this week's WORDS TO LIVE BY.

3. Can anyone of your peers reach that far?

DAY THREE: READ *YOU ARE LOVED*

1. Write out Romans 8:38-39.

2. Remember this when you are tempted to believe, *No one loves me, no one cares!*

DAY FOUR: READ *YOU ARE LOVED*

Nick was devastated over the behavior of his peers toward him. His mom knew that Nick needed encouraging, therefore she lovingly and carefully instructed him in the truth.

1. What did Nick's mom want him to understand about his peers?

2. What did Nick's mom want him to understand about God?

3. Memorize Psalm 136:1.

DAY FIVE: *LIVE IT!*

Everyone is different and everyone is good at something. List all the negative thoughts you have had about yourself and then try to turn those thoughts into something positive about yourself. For example: "I am a horrible athlete" is negative, but it could be turned into a positive thought by saying, "I am a really good artist".

PRAYER

Heavenly Father,

When I am tempted to believe No one loves me, no one cares, help me to remember the truth of your Word and give you thanks for your enduring love.

In Jesus' Name,
Amen

LIVING OUT GOD'S WORD!

_____

_____

_____

_____

_____

_____

_____

_____

_____

_____

_____

_____

_____

_____

_____

_____

THE AUTHORS

CAROLINE STOERKER AND HER GRANDMOTHER, ELLIE KRAUSE

Caroline Stoerker had just turned twelve years old when she first published **Alive in Him.** She lives in the Atlanta suburbs with her mom, dad, younger sister, and pet fish, Finn. She attends Piney Grove Middle School and there, is a percussionist in the seventh grade band and is a member of the audition-only, girls-only, Bel Canto chorus. She attends First Redeemer Church in Cumming and there she is involved in a small group and By All Means, a student worship team at the church. Her hobbies are singing, reading, writing, playing the piano, and hanging out with friends and family. Caroline is so excited about writing her first book and is very thankful to all her family and friends for their love and support!!!

Ellie Krause is Caroline's Nana. She lives in Rock Hill, South Carolina and is a member of Westminster Presbyterian church. She has written and taught Bible studies over the years. In her free time she enjoys walking, spending time with her husband, her three grown children, their spouses and her grandchildren.

To find our more about the authors, Caroline Stoerker or Ellie Krause, visit their web site at www.carolinestoerker.com.

To order additional copies of *Alive in Him*, for retail, ministry, education or fund raising or if you have a book in you contact Zoe Life at info@zoelifepub.com.

For more books that can change your world visit www.zoelifepub.com.

Zoë Life Publishing
P.O. Box 871066
Canton, MI 48187
(877) 841-3400
outreach@zoelifepub.com